The CAPE MAY NAVY

DELAWARE BAY PRIVATEERS IN THE AMERICAN REVOLUTION

J.P. HAND & DANIEL P. STITES

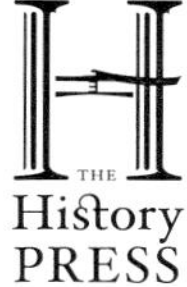

THE History PRESS

Published by The History Press
Charleston, SC
www.historypress.com

First published 2018

Manufactured in the United States

ISBN 9781467137966

Library of Congress Control Number: 2017963919

Notice: The information in this book is true and complete to the best of our knowledge. It is offered without guarantee on the part of the authors or The History Press. The authors and The History Press disclaim all liability in connection with the use of this book.

CONTENTS

PREFACE

Considerable research has gone into the writing of this text. As not all facts are annotated and documented, the authors would like to give the readers more information about the sources that have been used to compile this volume. Internet search engines such as Google and others were often helpful in identifying further sources. Genealogical sites such as Ancestry and Family Search were utilized in compiling family relationships. Additional internet sites used extensively were Fold 3 and GenBank. The latter was especially helpful in locating contemporary newspaper articles regarding the privateers of Cape May. The many books and other materials are indicated in the bibliography. Other sources include ledger books and personal letters from the Historical Society of Pennsylvania, the Cape May County Museum of History and Genealogy, the Library at Winterthur and Rowan University Library in Glassboro, New Jersey. The Cape May County Quarterly Court records from the Records Room at the Cape May County Clerk's Office and the Cumberland County Quarterly Court records held at the New Jersey State Archives were a wealth of information.

Some original and heretofore undiscovered records were uncovered and are extensively quoted in the book. Especially important was a receipt book (1774–83) of Colonel Richard Somers in the collection of one of the authors (JPH). Surviving headstones from cemeteries and family burial grounds in Cape May County also aided us in our research. Additional records regarding some of the Cape May privateer families are in private collections and were often consulted. We have given credit to the numerous sources for images used in the book.

In quotes excerpted from original eighteenth- and nineteenth-century documents we have preserved the spelling as written. Spelling in the colonies and early United States was often phonetic. Monetary units in colonial America were pounds, shillings and pence. Soon after achieving independence, some states adopted dollars, while others still maintained the British system. Unfortunately, it is difficult to convert any of these monetary values into currency of today. Many states did not conform to a federal standard until the nineteenth century. Estimating the value of currency is further complicated by the extensive counterfeiting of American currency by the British. The reader should refer to values given for goods and services to get an approximate idea of their actual worth. Certainly, thousands of pounds—which was not uncommon to retrieve from prizes taken at sea—were a substantial sum in the eighteenth century.

CAPE MAY NAVY
TIMELINE

1773

December | Cape May pilots refuse to bring up the Bay any tea ships of the East India Company

1774

January | Delaware Bay pilots are warned not to escort British tea ships into port through a series of letters printed in contemporary newspapers and signed, "Your old friends, The Committee for tarring and feathering, Philadelphia"

November | Jesse Hand Esq. delivers to Philadelphia "a genteel sum of money" raised by the citizens of Cape May to be sent to the "suffering poor" of Boston in response to the British enactment of the Intolerable Acts

1775

June 17 | Battle of Bunker Hill

September 21 | The inhabitants of Cape May County vote in the affirmative to raise a battalion of militia and elect militia officers

1776

April 3	Congress issues initial orders for letters of marque
June 29	Battle of Turtle Gut Inlet
September 15	The British take New York
December 26	Battle of Trenton (Hessian captain Andreas Wiederholdt captured)

1777

July	Cape May investors Aaron Leaming Jr., John Holmes Sr. and Jesse Hand expand their saltworks at Seven Mile Beach (Stone Harbor/Avalon)
September 26	The British take Philadelphia
October 22	American forces repulse Hessian attack on Fort Mercer (Battle of Red Bank), Gloucester County

1778

Thomas Leaming Jr., John Holmes Sr., Enoch Stillwell, Jesse Hand and other investors of Cape May and Great Egg Harbour begin to purchase and outfit privateer vessels

March 18	Lieutenant Colonel and privateer captain Elijah Hand and his Cumberland Militia drive British troops from Quinton's Bridge, Salem County
June 18	The British depart from Philadelphia
June–July	Yelverton Taylor captures the brig *Liberty* and the schooner *Phoenix*

September — Captain Moses Griffing captures the sloop *George*; Captain Enoch Stillwell takes the *Marydunceo*; Captain Yelverton Taylor, in the privateer sloop *Comet*, takes the schooners *Fame*, *Hannah*, *Caroline* and *Good Intent*

October 6 — British and Loyalist landing parties burn the privateer port of Chestnut Neck, Gloucester County (Battle of Chestnut Neck)

October–December — Captain Moses Griffing takes the sloop *Commerce* and schooner *Rambler*

November — Captain Humphrey Hughes and his twenty-five-man crew aboard the privateer sloop *New Comet* disappear on what was allegedly the vessel's maiden voyage

1779

June — In an open boat called the *Skunk*, John Goldin, with twelve men and two guns (small cannons), captures his nineteenth prize

September — In the privateer schooner *Hawk*, Captain Enoch Stillwell captures the brig *Lyon* and schooner *Henry*; British brig *Triton*, with a Hessian regiment on board, departs Sandy Hook, New Jersey; in the privateer sloop *Mars*, Captain Yelverton Taylor takes *Triton* (with Captain Wiederholdt on board)

November — Privateer officer Matthew Hand sues Captain Enoch Stillwell for nonpayment of his £3,000 share of prizes; litigation of the *Lyon* and *Henry* capture by the privateer schooner *Hawk*

1780

April	In the schooner *Rattlesnake*, Captain William Treen takes the prize sloop *Dispatch*, or *Speedwell*
May 2	Congress issues *Instructions to Privateers* (See Appendix Item 5)

1781

January	In the brig *Fame*, William Treen captures the refugee privateer *Cock*
January 22	The privateer *Fame*, overset in a gale while "lying in Egg Harbour," loses twenty-five crewmen
June	Captain Aaron Swain recaptures the *General Greene*
October 19	Battle of Yorktown, British surrender

1782

April 8	American privateer *HyderAlly* takes the British warship *General Monk* in Delaware Bay off of Cape May
May	In the armed boats *Enterprize* and *Quick-Time*, Elijah Hand and Enoch Willets drive ashore the refugee boat *Old Ranger* near Little Egg Harbor
April–July	Captain John Badcock recaptures the schooners *Anney* and *Polly*
May–September	In the armed boat *Black Joke*, Hope Willets retakes the schooners *Albenus* and *Flying-Fish*

| June | In the armed boats *Black Joke* and *Luck and Fortune*, Captain Hope Willets and Captain Joseph Edwards retake the sloop *Nancy*, which had been captured by the British cruiser *Fair American* |
| August | Captain John Badcock recaptures the schooner *Hawke* |

1783

March	Captain Joseph Edwards recaptures the schooner *Susannah*, "lately captured by the British schooner *Dragon*"
September 3	The Treaty of Paris brings the Revolutionary War to an end
November 25	The British depart New York

1780–86

Revolutionary War prize cases heard by Admiralty Courts of Pennsylvania and New Jersey

1832

Aged Cape May privateer crewmen who were teenagers during their service in the Revolution apply for war pensions as authorized by Congress in 1832, including:
Jeremiah Hand
Henry Izard
Recompence Hand
Nathaniel Holmes
Shamgar Hewitt
Jacob Garretson (moved to Indiana)

INTRODUCTION

J.P. HAND

As the editor of the annual *Cape May County Magazine of History and Genealogy*, or "Blue Book," as it is known, I am always on the lookout for topics or subjects regarding our local history that haven't been given their due. I have found that in the eighty-six years of publication of our journal, many important stories in our county's history have never been covered or have been only mentioned ever so briefly.

In past years, my distant cousin and friend Dr. Daniel Page Stites has contributed a number of articles for publication. One of Dan's articles featured two celebrated Delaware Bay pilots, father and son Matthew Hand (1754–1828) and Page Stites (1791–1867). In 2009, while doing research for and discussing that article with Dan, I suggested that another good topic for him to tackle was the story of the men of Cape May County who served as privateers during the American Revolution.

A year earlier, I had written an article for the Blue Book chronicling the life of Cape May native Colonel Elijah Hand. During the Revolution and in the following decades, Elijah Hand was known throughout the country due to the publication of his eloquent reply to the threatening letter sent to him by British commander Colonel Charles Mawhood shortly after the skirmish at Quinton's Bridge in Salem County, New Jersey (see chapter 9).

While researching details of Colonel Hand's life, it became obvious to me that he was almost as well known as a privateer captain as he was as a militia colonel. Further research led to an article, "A Matter of Definition:

A New Jersey Navy, 1777–1783," by the U.S. Coast Guard historian, Dr. Robert L. Scheina, published in *American Neptune, A Quarterly Journal of Maritime History* (July 1979). The premise of Dr. Scheina's article was a response to a statement by one of the most esteemed naval historians of the American Revolution, Gardiner Allen, who wrote, "[T]he sentiment of local independence and the loose federation of the colonies…naturally led to individual action…so that, in addition to the Continental Navy, eleven of the thirteen states maintained armed vessels, New Jersey and Delaware being the exceptions." As Dr. Scheina put it, "Today, there is adequate evidence to prove the existence of a New Jersey navy." Much of Scheina's argument is based on the exploits of privateer captain Elijah Hand and the pension applications of some of his Cape May crewmen, including his son, Recompence Hand.

In hindsight, it is easy to see why Gardiner Allen would make such a statement, as most of the available official records on the subject, including the Library of Congress's *Naval Records of the American Revolution 1775–1788*, lists (with the exception of one) all of Cape May's privateer vessel owners, masters and mates as being from Philadelphia. This can be explained by the fact that all of the vessels owned or commanded by Cape May men were issued letters of marque (that is, the license to attack and capture enemy ships) in that city.

On the other hand, most contemporary newspaper accounts list those same captains and vessels as "of Cape May" or "[Great] Egg Harbour" and so on. It became obvious that anyone without a general knowledge of the history and people who settled on the Cape and the adjoining counties of Salem and Cumberland and the Great Egg Harbor portion of Gloucester (now Atlantic County) would make the same assertion that Gardiner Allen had.

One postwar letter, from Cape May's Thomas Leaming Jr. to the Honorable William Paterson (New Jersey senator and later governor), helps to illustrate the importance of Cape May's privateers to the war effort and the economy of Cape May County (see Item 4 in the appendix). In that letter, dated February 17, 1789, Leaming appealed to fellow lawyer and patriot Paterson to support him in his quest to be appointed to a position in the Federal Court at Philadelphia.

The following excerpt not only reveals the scope of Leaming's involvement in privateering but also gives us a sense of the scale of the participation of the men of Cape May:

> [A]*s I was concerned in the Importation of Considerable Quantities of Ammunition, Salt, and other Necessaries, and also in the Capture of near 50 Prizes large and small in which more than 1000 Prisoners were taken, which served to exchange for American Prisoners in the Hands of the Enemy. By one of the Privateers, which I built and held a principle share in, about 500 Hessian-English Soldiers were taken in there Vessels within a few days. This would have been deemed an Acquisition by the Army even if they lost half the number in affecting it and yet it did not cost the Life of a Man or the Publick, One Shilling.*

Over the course of four or five years, Dr. Stites and I spent many hours gleaning information from various sources, including U.S. Naval records, newspaper accounts and court records, as well as the private journals and ledgers of some of the privateer owner-investors themselves. Ultimately, that research revealed that a good portion of the fifty enemy vessels mentioned in Thomas Leaming's letter were captured by Cape May privateer captains. The letter also answered the question as to why most of the Cape May privateers who were captured and held in squalor on board the prison hulks of New York were routinely exchanged, some on multiple occasions.

Not long into the project we realized that the story was much bigger and much more complicated than we had imagined. Before long, we decided that this incredible story concerning Cape May County's part in the founding of our nation deserved more than a brief article on the subject.

In his article, Dr. Robert Scheina was successful in setting the record straight regarding the existence of armed vessels from the state of New Jersey that fought in the American Revolution. Ultimately, the goal of Dr. Stites and me was to bring to light the complicated story of the men and vessels of the Cape May Navy. The results of our mutual efforts are to be found in this volume.

D.P. STITES

THE IDEA FOR THIS BOOK about the Cape May Navy emerged from many conversations James P. Hand and I had about ten years ago concerning the history of the county. We knew we wanted to research and write about some interesting and novel facts about Revolutionary War history in Cape

May and eventually focused on the sea war. James Hand and I are distant cousins and both descended from the Hand brothers—Shamgar, Thomas and Benjamin—who all migrated from Long Island to Cape May in the late seventeenth century. Our collaboration has always been and will continue to be a source of deep and abiding pleasure to us both.

There is no doubt that the Revolution was to a large extant won on the sea and, of course, not by the regular navy—which for America was embryonic at best—but by private warships commanded by young privateers. These men were not pirates, as some think, but generally those with letters of marque from the Continental Congress, which gave them the legal right to attack, board and capture ships of the enemy—the British. There were many ports along the East Coast that served as havens for these ships and their crews. Prominent among them were Baltimore, New York, Boston and Philadelphia. Cape May itself did not serve as a sea port, as it does not have readily accessible deep water anchorage. Nevertheless, as we will point out in this book, the men and boys of Cape May County played a considerable role in the naval war. Most of them, including the captains, were in their twenties. Many of them shipped from Philadelphia, and some sailed from Great Egg Harbor around what is now Tuckahoe. Little Egg Harbor and Barnegat Bay served as havens where captured British vessels were taken by privateers and then transshipped to places near Philadelphia to be sold as prizes. The crew then benefitted substantially from such sales and, in some cases, became rich. Although privateering could be a very lucrative business for the sailors, it was also very dangerous. Being captured meant incarceration on prison ships under horrible conditions in Brooklyn Harbor (Wallabout Bay) or, worse yet, the Old Mill Prison near Plymouth, England.

Some of what we have found and related here is original research with documented primary sources. This is especially true of the small journal of Colonel Richard Somers, who played a major role as "the banker" of Cape May privateers. His dwelling was in what is now Somers Point in Atlantic (then Gloucester) County right across the Egg Harbor River from Cape May County. It is still standing. Also remarkable is the interrelatedness of many of the privateers. This is well documented in chapter 3, "Family Business." The familial relationships are not surprising, as in the late eighteenth century, Cape May County had only a few thousand in population. One of the most interesting figures in our narrative is Yelverton Taylor, about whom we know very little. He seems to have been in his twenties and a master privateer. An exciting narrative of the events leading up to his capture of Andreas Wiederholdt and a ship full of Hessians is detailed in chapter 5, "The Wiederholdt Affair." Included in this chapter are reproductions of original colored drawings by Captain Wiederholdt of his tattered ship and the two privateer vessels captained by Yelverton Taylor and Stephen Decatur Sr. that caught him off Absecon Island.

We hope that this narrative will add substance to the many books and articles that have been written about the American Revolution and, more specifically, the history of Cape May County.

In relation to the characters in this text, author Dan Stites is a direct descendant of the pilot and privateer Matthew Hand, while J.P. Hand is a direct descendant of privateer captains Colonel Elijah Hand and Lieutenant Colonel Enoch Stillwell. Both authors are direct descendants of privateer officer Nathaniel Holmes Sr.

1

THE UNTOLD STORY

J.P. HAND

THE STORY OF THE PRIVATEERS of Cape May County is one of the many unrecorded or underreported chapters in that county's history. One detail that sets this story apart from other privateer tales is the disproportionate contribution toward the fight for independence made by the Cape's mariner-soldiers in relation to the small population of the county.

Cape May's earliest European settlers arrived in the late seventeenth century, primarily from eastern and western Long Island, East Jersey and New England. These whaler-yeomen were drawn to the Cape by the lucrative whaling industry and large tracts of relatively inexpensive land. By the mid-eighteenth century, the whaling grounds at Cape May had been depleted, and the remaining primary export industries were, in order of importance: livestock, timber, oysters and the strictly female cottage industry of producing woolen mittens and stockings for export.

With the outbreak of hostilities between the British and their American subjects, the conditions at Cape May (and its neighboring counties) were conducive to the enterprise of privateering. The Cape May peninsula was strategically located (by sea) between Philadelphia and New York; both cities were occupied by the British for part of the war. Surrounded by water on three sides, situated between the Atlantic Ocean and the Delaware Bay, the county is only about ten miles wide by thirty miles long. Despite an estimated population of only about two thousand souls in 1775, many of the county's men were either full- or part-time mariners: ship captains,

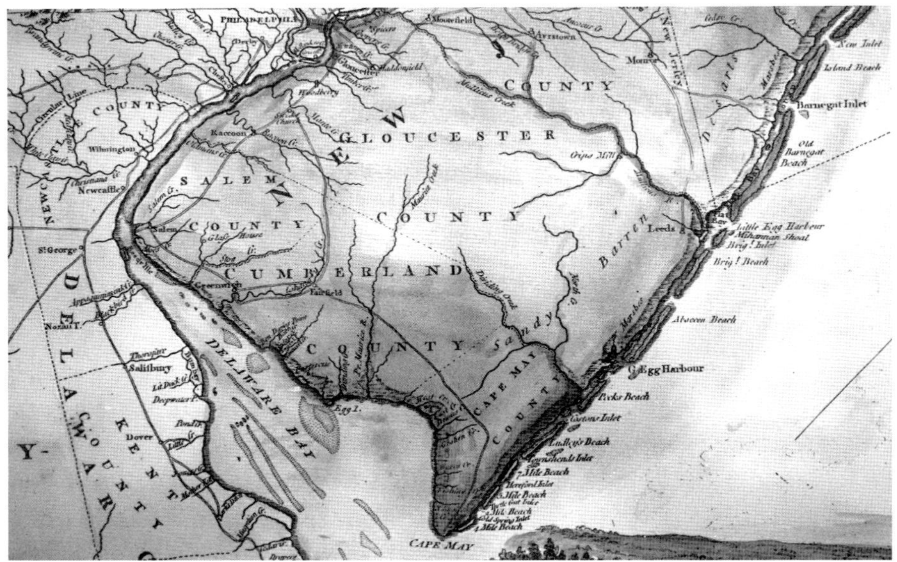

Holland-Pownall Map of Cape May and surrounding counties, 1776. *J.P. Hand collection.*

crewmen or members of that most exclusive fraternity, the Delaware Bay pilots. Many of them were what we today refer to as "baymen," making at least a part of their livelihood off of the water (see appendix Item 1).

Most of these men had grown up gunning for waterfowl and harvesting oysters and clams on the county's tidal wetlands on the sounds of the seaside or the bayside of the Cape. They were familiar with the intricacies of the ever-changing contours of the inlets, bays, channels and sandbars—knowledge that would serve them well when trying to avoid any British or Refugee (Tory) vessels that outgunned them. Many of the county's wealthier plantation owners owned or invested in privateer vessels and employed their relatives and neighbors to man them.

In other words, within two generations, the men of Cape May County had transitioned from hunting whales to hunting British merchant vessels and, when possible, British naval vessels as well. Just as their fathers and grandfathers had fished the waters of the Atlantic Ocean and the Delaware Bay for whales, Cape May's privateers searched for a different kind of prey in those same waters.

In an almost "perfect storm" scenario, the pieces were all in place for the development of this patriotic and potentially lucrative industry. Most

PHILADELPHIA.

From the beft authority we learn that the ftate of Maryland hath agreed to the confederation of the United States, by which means the confederacy is now compleat.

We alfo learn that the ftate of Virginia have given up their claim to the back lands, and have, in a formal manner, by a law, ceded to the United States all the lands lying to the weftward of the River Ohio.

The brig Fame, Capt. Treen, about fourteen days ago, took the privateer fchooner Cock, Capt. Brooks, bound from New-York on a cruize to Chefapeak Bay, and fent her into a port in New-Jerfey.

We hear the brig Fame, Capt. Treen, lying in Egg-Harbour, in the gale of wind on the 22d inftant, was overfet, and it is faid twenty-five of her hands were drowned.

Report of the *Fame* overturned. *Courtesy of the American Antiquarian Society.*

of Cape May's privateer investors were merchants involved in the import-export trade. These men put up the capital to purchase and outfit privateer vessels and knew how and where to dispose of the prizes and their cargoes, all the while keeping the same out of the reach of the British.

Many of the county's younger men (reportedly as young as thirteen years of age) and more mature citizens with little assets were more than willing to serve as crewmen on privateer vessels on the chance of making their fortune or at least improving their lot in life. They chose to serve despite the dangers, including running the risk of dying in battle, being lost at sea or drowned in storms or capture and imprisonment on one of the notorious prison ships in British-occupied New York (see appendix Item 3).

As for Cape May's shipmasters, mariners and Delaware Bay pilots, they often served as privateer captains, mates and, in the case of larger vessels, first or second officers. It is important to note that a high number of Cape May's privateers also served in various militia units at some point during the war. This dual service suggests that their motivation was a combination of patriotic fervor and the enticement of prize money. It is also notable that the record shows that certain Cape May families seemed to have shouldered the burden entirely, while other early and prominent families of the county are noticeably absent from the militia rolls and lists of privateer officers and crewmen (see chapter 3, "Family Business").

The same scenario was taking place up and down the Eastern Seaboard: locally owned and manned vessels were outfitted for war against what was arguably the greatest navy the world had ever seen. While technically British subjects, the residents of Cape May appear to have had little qualms about shedding their allegiance to England, and it can be said that the county was almost completely committed to the struggle for independence. This didn't hold true for counties to the north, in the pine barrens of old Burlington County or the rolling farmland of Monmouth County, where Patriots not only had to fear the British forces but also the depredations of those of their neighbors who had chosen to remain loyal to the Crown. These Loyalists, or Tories as they were known on land, were most often referred to as "Refugees" when operating at sea.

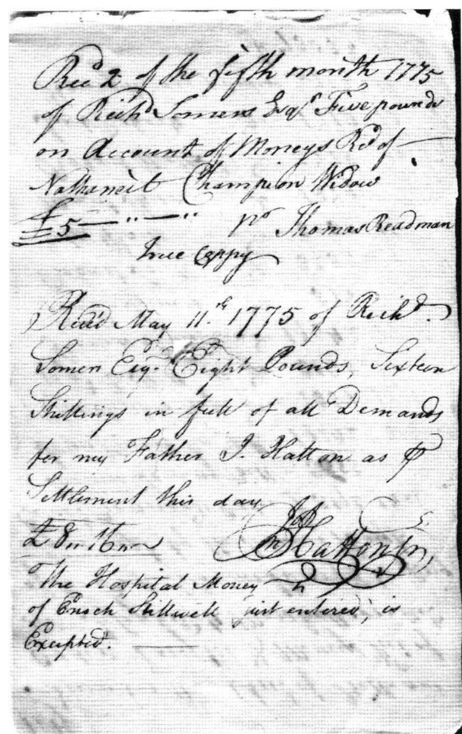

Left: A 1775 payment to the despised royal customs collector John Hatton from Richard Somers's receipt book. *Private collection.*

Below: The news report of Cape May politician Jesse Hand's visit to Philadelphia reveals his county's response to the harsh treatment that the inhabitants of Massachusetts received from the British, *Connecticut Courant* (Hartford), November 21, 1774. *Courtesy of the American Antiquarian Society.*

> ### PHILADELPHIA, Nov. 14.
> We are informed that a few days ago Jeſſe Hand, Eſq; of Cape May, came to this city with a genteel ſum of money, generouſly ſubſcribed by the people of that place, to be laid out for the uſe of the ſuffering poor of Boſton.

Throughout the thirteen original colonies, Loyalists had their property confiscated during and after the war. Remarkably, no resident of Cape May County and only two absentee landowners had their land confiscated by the new government. The first, John Hatton, was the despised Royal customs collector, who had had previous run-ins and disputes with many of Cape May's merchants and sea captains over their refusal to pay import duties. The following transcription of a legal notice posted in Trenton's *New-Jersey Gazette* details how that process took place:

State of New-Jersey,
Cape May county.

Whereas inquisition was found, and final judg-ment entered in favour of the state of New-Jersey, in the county of Gloucester, in December term, 1778, against John Hatton, late of said county of Gloucester, collector of the customs to the King of Great-Britain:

Notice is hereby given,
That in pursuance of such judgment, and in virtue of the act of Assembly in the case provided, all the lands; tenements and estate, of said John Hatton, which can be found in the county of Cape-May aforesaid, will be exposed to sale, at a publick vendue, on Saturday the 29ᵗʰ of May next, at the house of Thomas Buck, innkeeper in the Lower Precinct of said county; where attendance will be given by JESSE HAND, Agent of forfeited estates for said county.
April 23, 1784

N.B. Gold and silver money, officers' and soldiers' notes given for depreciation of their pay, contractors' certificates, and collector' surplus certificates, will be taken in payment for said estates.
April 23, 1784.

The second individuals to have property in Cape May County confiscated were the heirs of Dr. Daniel Coxe, who had been the proprietary governor of West Jersey and the largest landowner of that province from 1687 to 1692. Those heirs, Daniel Coxe Esq. and John Tabor-Kempe (husband of Grace Coxe), lost lands throughout New Jersey and New York as well.

If any of Cape May's residents had Loyalist inclinations, they kept those feelings to themselves. In contrast, though neighboring Cumberland County could boast a large population of Patriots, the Cumberland County Quarterly Court records reveal a surprisingly large number of residents being charged with various acts of disloyalty to the new Republic. The offenses included "disaffection to the government, crossing enemy lines, piloting the enemy, and treason."

It should be noted that this story could not properly be told without the inclusion of many of the mariner-soldiers in the counties bordering Cape May, including Cumberland County to the northwest and particularly coastal Gloucester County, New Jersey (now Atlantic County). The

Elizabeth-Town, April 19, 1784.   3w†

State of New-Jersey, ⎫ WHEREAS inquisition was
Cape-May county, ⎬ found, and final judgment entered in favour of the state of New-Jersey, in the county of Gloucester, in December term, 1778, against John Hatton, late of said county of Gloucester, collector of the customs to the King of Great-Britain:

Notice is hereby given,

That in pursuance of such judgment, and in virtue of the act of Assembly in that case provided, all the lands, tenements and estate, of said John Hatton, which can be found in the county of Cape-May aforesaid, will be exposed to sale, at publick vendue, on Saturday the 29th of May next, at 11 o'clock in the forenoon, at the house of Thomas Buck, innkeeper in the Lower Precinct of said county; where attendance will be given by   JESSE HAND, Agent of forfeited estates for said county.

N. B. Gold and silver money, officers' and soldiers' notes given for depreciation of their pay, contractors' certificates, and collectors' surplus certificates, will be taken in payment for said estates.

April 23, 1784.   4w‖

Above: Legal notice advertising the sale of the forfeited estate of British customs collector John Hatton, *New-Jersey Gazette*, April 26, 1784. *Courtesy of the American Antiquarian Society.*

Right: Elijah Matthews, killed while serving on board the privateer schooner *Mars* (Captain Yelverton Taylor), old burial ground, (CMC Park) Cape May Court House, New Jersey. *Photo by Jim Talone.*

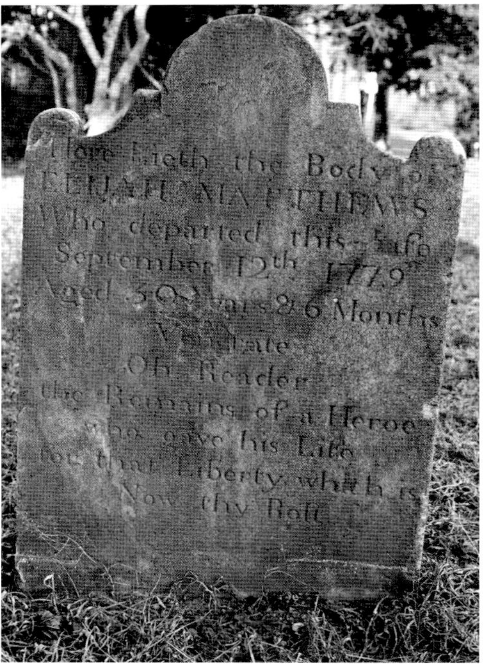

merchants, mariners and militiamen from all three counties who had a vested interest in privateering were not only connected culturally but in many cases through family and business ties as well.

One final note: up until the mid-nineteenth century, the City of Cape May was known as Cape Island, while the term "Cape May" was used in reference to anywhere on the Jersey Cape. Accordingly, throughout this text, the authors have used that traditional term to denote anywhere in Cape May County.

2

THE NATURE, REWARDS AND DANGERS OF BEING A PRIVATEER

D.P. STITES

Privateering is usually defined as a type of naval warfare conducted in privately owned ships in contrast to a government-owned and operated navy. Permits to conduct private warfare are called letters of marque (LOM) or marque and reprisal and were licenses issued by governments to private citizens. Originally, they were used by individuals to garner restitution from offending parties by various rulers. The first LOM was probably issued in Tuscany in the twelfth century. England issued LOM from the thirteenth century onward, and the practice was adopted by the American Continental Congress and guaranteed in the U.S. Constitution (Article 1, Section 8).

> *Congress shall have the Power…to declare War, issue Letters of Marque and Reprisal and make Rules concerning Captures on Land and Water.*

Specific instructions regarding the behavior of privateers fighting in the Revolution were passed in Congress in 1780–81 (see Appendix Item 5, "Instruction to Privateers from Congress 1780–81").

The phrase *letter of marque* also refers to a cargo ship clandestinely or openly armed with a license to capture enemy ships. The main distinction between a pirate and a privateer was this license. Of course, there were many other distinctions as well, but privateering was a totally legal pursuit guaranteed by the laws of the land, whereas pirating was clearly illegal. Strictly speaking, privateer ships were armed vessels of war, usually smaller ships like sloops

IN CONGRESS.

The DELEGATES of the UNITED COLONIES of *New-Hampshire, Massachusetts-Bay, Rhode-Island, Connecticut, New-York, New-Jersey, Pennsylvania,* the Counties of *New-Castle, Kent* and *Sussex* on *Delaware, Maryland, Virginia, North-Carolina, South-Carolina,* and *Georgia,* TO All unto whom these Presents shall come, send GREETING: KNOW YE,

THAT we have granted, and by these Presents do grant Licence and Authority to   Mariner, Commander of the   called   of the Burthen of   Tons, or thereabouts, belonging to   of   in the Colony of   mounting   Carriage Guns, and navigated by   Men, to fit out and set forth the said   in a warlike Manner, and by and with the said   and the Crew thereof, by Force of Arms, to attack, seize, and take the Ships and other Vessels belonging to the Inhabitants of Great-Britain, or any of them, with their Tackle, Apparel, Furniture and Ladings, on the High Seas, or between high-water and low-water Marks, and to bring the same to some convenient Ports in the said Colonies, in Order that the Courts, which are or shall be there appointed to hear and determine Causes civil and maritime, may proceed in due Form to condemn the said Captures, if they be adjudged lawful Prize; the said   having given Bond, with sufficient Sureties, that Nothing be done by the said   or any of the Officers, Mariners or Company thereof contrary to, or inconsistent with the Usages and Customs of Nations, and the Instructions, a Copy of which is herewith delivered to him. And we will and require all our Officers whatsoever to give Succour and Assistance to the said   in the Premises. This Commission shall continue in Force until the Congress shall issue Orders to the Contrary.

By Order of the Congress,

Dated at   *John Hancock* PRESIDENT.

Letter of marque from the Revolutionary War. *Courtesy of Firestone Library, Princeton University.*

or schooners with only a few guns but often a crew of nearly fifty or more. American privateering was essentially limited to the two wars against Great Britain, and these warriors dominated the sea campaigns.

Privateering was abandoned after the Paris Declaration Respecting Maritime Law of 1856, of which the United States was *not* a signatory. The country has never been party to a treaty renouncing privateering. However, by convention, America has observed the Declaration of Paris, but in 2007–9, Congressman Ron Paul (R-Texas) unsuccessfully tried to reinstitute the practice in Congress to combat terrorism and specifically Somali pirates.

American privateering was a major military and economic activity during the Revolution. According to Patton, privateering was a large boon to the American economy through shipbuilding, employment of individuals involved in outfitting and selling prize wares and wild speculation on privateering trade itself. Huge fortunes were made and lost. While the American land forces mainly held out against superior British army troops, privateers took a much more aggressive stance and actually took the war to the British. In so doing, they humiliated the Crown and severely threatened the British public.

Parliament passed an act to combat privateering, the Treason Act, in 1777, relegating American privateering to an illegal action (piracy) supported by an illegitimate Congress. Prisoners were to be held without trial and placed in woeful conditions in mainland and American prisons. British subjects were often outraged at this position and attempted both legal and prison reforms in support of the colonists. Franklin further exacerbated the anger of the English by secretly encouraging the sale of British prizes in French ports, which was a breach of neutrality.

The British licensed about eight hundred privateers during the War for Independence, while the colonists had seven hundred letters of marque active all over the Atlantic and Caribbean. The major privateer ports were Boston, Providence, New York (totally British), Baltimore and, of course, Philadelphia and the coast of South Jersey. In 1777, the British capture of Philadelphia temporarily ended that port's role in privateering until the British abandoned the city in June 1778. Privateering supplanted government-funded navies in many instances due to the enormous expense of shipbuilding and outfitting. Only one letter of marque was issued in New Jersey (New Brunswick), but twenty-one issued in Philadelphia included most of those with Cape May connections. Letters of marque were often issued by port commissioners acting on behalf of states or the federal government. Records of many of these were either not kept or have been unfortunately lost. Specific instructions to privateers were issued in a declaration by the Continental Congress on April 3, 1776, amended in 1780, and are reproduced in the appendix, Item 5, in full.

Investment in privateers was a high risk–high reward venture. Of course, patriotism may also have been a motivating factor for owning private warships. Thomas Leaming, originally of Cape May and a lawyer-businessman who worked with the firm of Bunner and Company in Philadelphia, owned more than fifty privateers and clearly made a large fortune during the war. Building a two-hundred-ton schooner cost approximately $40,000 in 1813—prices the equivalent of $400,000 or more today. Investment partnerships were common, with shares of $1,000 to $4,000 per investor. Enemy ships captured at sea were the property of the owners and crew, who had the ships condemned in admiralty courts and sold at auction. All of the proceeds were divided usually evenly between the crew and the owners. The owners were required by American law to post bond of about $5,000 to $10,000 per ship, depending on tonnage, to ensure that seafaring laws would be observed. The state and federal governments did not get a share. Initially, 50 percent of prizes taken by the regular navy, however, belonged to Congress, but later this was reduced to a third to encourage prize capture. Captains and crew could sell their shares to the owners.

The crews of American privateers were plentiful and recruited from seagoing areas like South Jersey. Many crewmen were landlubbers, but not those from the maritime county of Cape May. Many were in their twenties or younger—rarely forty or older. Crew members worked for incentive pay only but often shared quite nicely if several ships were captured. It was a dangerous but lucrative undertaking. Shares were apportioned according to rank. Extra shares were often added for sighting ships or loss of limb or other injuries sustained in the chase. Food and drink were plentiful, and being a crew member on a privateer was much more popular than serving in the regular navy. There was, of course, no general recognition for a privateer's success, and no pensions were awarded until after 1813. Nevertheless, these men often showed surprising acts of bravery.

The consequences of getting captured by an enemy vessel were often disastrous for the crew and officers of American privateers. The British did not generally recognize American privateers as such and considered them pirates. They were not hanged, as actual pirates were, but suffered immeasurably in Forton and Mill Prisons, Portsmouth and seven rotting prison ships in Wallabout Bay, Brooklyn, New York.

It is estimated that more than three thousand American sailors were imprisoned in England. About one thousand were exchanged, and as many as thirteen thousand died. Estimates suggest only about eight hundred Continental navy seamen were captured, but untold numbers of privateers died in combat. The conditions on prison ships were not equaled in cruelty until the American Civil War and, notably, Nazi German concentration

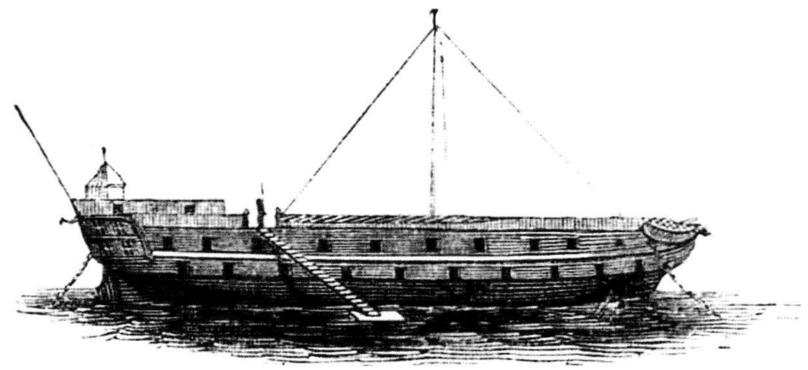

Prison ship *Jersey. Library of Congress.*

camps centuries later. As many as eight thousand men were imprisoned on the prison ship *Jersey* in Brooklyn, many of whom died from the horrible treatment. Food and sanitation were essentially absent, and every day, corpses were thrown overboard or buried on the sandy beach. In 1888, a monument was erected in Green Park, Brooklyn, to the Patriots who died in Wallabout Bay. Several names on the list of prisoners belong to Cape May privateers.

DEFINITE

Elijah Hand
Nathaniel Holmes
Enoch Stillwell
John Stillwell
William Treen
James Willets
Joseph Wheaton

POSSIBLE

James Holmes
John & Henry Ingersoll
David, James, Joseph Ireland
Simon (Simeon?) Swain
Zachariah Swain
Parmenas Corson

Each day at least six carcasses we bore,
And scratched their graves along the sandy shore:
By feeble hands the shallow graves were made,
No stone memorial o'er the corpses laid.
In barren sands and far from home they lie,
No friend to shed a tear when passing by;
O'er the mean tombs insulting Britons tread,
Spurn at the sand and curse the rebel dead
—From National Magazine, A Monthly Journal of American History *vol. 19, 1893*

A graphic example of suffering on prison ships is provided in the 1830 Revolutionary War pension application of John Ingersoll, a New Jersey privateer captured and imprisoned by the British. Thomas Leaming of Cape May and Philadelphia was responsible for freeing more than one thousand American prisoners through exchanges. While serving on a lookout boat off New Jersey, Ingersoll was captured and spent two months on a British hospital prison ship, the *Huntress*.

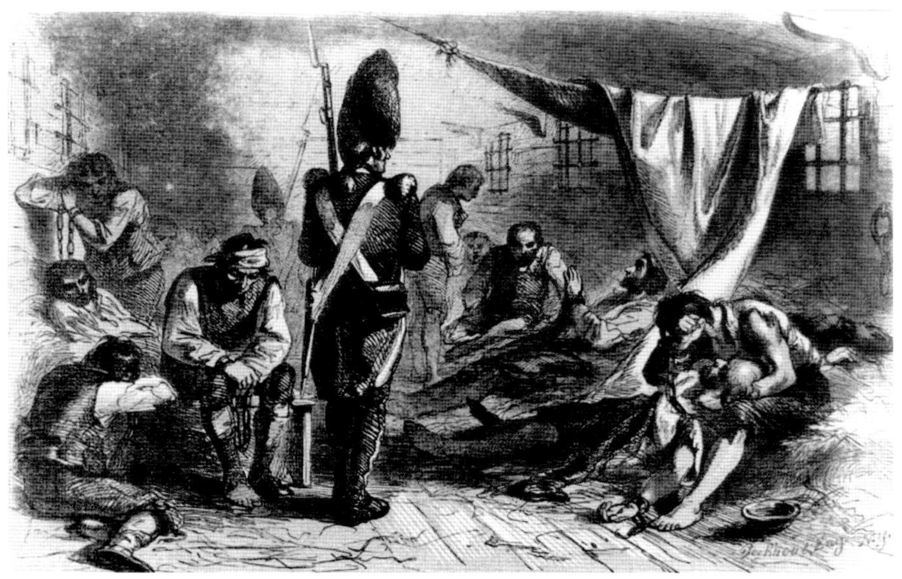

Interior of prison ship *Jersey. Library of Congress.*

John Ingersoll "We Laid a Plan for our Escape"

I remained on board the Scorpion *about three weeks. It being then in the month of July, I was taken sick with a camp fever, when I was removed out of the* Scorpion *and put on board the* Huntress, *also a prison ship but then converted into a hospital. I was on board the* Huntress *but a short time, when I was attacked with dysentery. Here I thought would be an end to my sufferings, but, although death relieved some of my messmates from the horrors of that prison (Captain Willets was among the number who fell a victim to the disease), I was one among those who recovered. The water was bad and the provisions worse. Our allowance was a half-pound of mutton per day, but, to our surprise, when the mutton came on board it was only the heads of sheep with the horns and wool thereon. Our bread was oatmeal, neither sifted nor bolted. Our manner of preparing it was as follows: pound up a sheep's head until the bones were all broken, then sink the oatmeal in a bowl of water and float out the hulls; with this we would thicken the broth and thus we kept soul and body together.*

I had been on board about two months, sometimes almost famished for the want of provisions, when the officers of the hospital ship made a proposal to me. In case I would keep the cabin clean, boil their teakettle, black their boots, etc., I should have a hammock to sleep in, should be better fed, and should be exchanged when the rest of my company was. I accordingly accepted of the offer. The hospital ship was anchored in what is called Buttermilk Channel with their cables and anchors. The center one was a tremendous chain cable. There were but one gun kept on board said ship, and that was an English musket which the officers kept in the cabin. There were about two hundred prisoners on board said ship, with seven officers and one physician.

I had been doing my duty in the cabin about two weeks, when we laid a plan for our escape. It was as follows. One day while the officers were absent on Long Island, I took down the said musket, poured out the priming, poured water in the barrel of the gun until the load became thoroughly wet. I then wiped the pan thoroughly dry, reprimed her, and put her back in her place. One or two days had elapsed, but we could get no boat wherein to make our escape, for they universally at night chained and locked her fast.

An opportunity at length presented itself, to wit, the officers had a mind to go on shore, and, it being tremendous stormy weather, they unlocked their boat from the chain, brought her up alongside, and ordered a boy to get into the boat and bail the water out of her. I had communicated the secret of the gun being out of order to some of my fellow prisoners, and there being at time a heavy storm, with the wind blowing directly upon the Jersey shore together with a thick, dense fog in the air, we considered this a favorable time to make our escape. We accordingly embraced the opportunity which then offered. National Humanities Center for Revolutionary War Pension Applications, 1830s, National Archives, Selections 9

Privateer vessels were generally small and fast sloops or schooners carrying four to ten guns and twenty to fifty men. Once a prize was spotted, the privateer often hoisted a false flag to avoid detection. The object was to capture, not destroy the prey. Fighting was only a last resort. British merchant ships often traveled in large convoys and were stalked by smaller American vessels that attacked in groups at night. First sighting by a privateer crewman often resulted in £100 bonuses. Gun battles occasionally ensued, and the cargo ships would usually strike their colors and surrender to the privateer vessel. Cargo ships would then be boarded, and fights erupted if the flags were not taken down.

Crew members from the privateer would then man the captured ship and take it into a port for condemnation and sale. The enemy crew was generally assigned to prisoner-of-war jails but sometimes volunteered to join the privateers as new crew members. Sometimes, the prisoners revolted and retook the ship. More often, they were exchanged for enemy prisoners of war.

Historical records strongly suggest that British officials and military officers were wholly responsible for the criminal conditions on these prison ships. Those mainly responsible were Provost Marshal William Cunningham, Commissary Joshua Larson and Naval Commissary David Sprout. Evidence for these conditions has come from letters and books written by prisoners and the report of Elias Boudinot, who was appointed by General Washington to secure the exchange or release of the prisoners (see appendix Item 6). Boudinot was a lawyer from Elizabeth, New Jersey who served as president of the Continental Congress in 1782–83. William Cunningham had been appointed by General William Howe and, according to Fish, was a "thoroughly vicious character" who was brought up in Ireland, the son of a British officer. He developed an intense hatred for American Rebels and was once beaten by a group of them called the Liberty Boys in New York. Cunningham later admitted that he was wholly responsible for the maltreatment of American captives and claimed he saw no reason not to have done so. According to Fish, Sprout was responsible for even more deaths than the Patriots executed by Joshua Loring and Cunningham. The death rate in the prison ships approached 85 percent, compared to about 15 percent in German World War II prison camps. Cunningham was convicted of forgery and executed in London in 1791. Prior to his death, he wrote a full confession of his misdeeds in New York. Cunningham's conviction/execution in 1791 is disputed.

Admiralty courts were initially state run but later became federal jurisdictions. In March 1776, after rather chaotic legal jurisdictional problems concerning privateers, admiralty courts were established in various states. Congress issued a critical proclamation formally stating that all British ships were fair game for capture either by the navy or privateers. The job of admiralty courts was to establish nationality of the prize using ship documents and testimony. Many of these trials were heard by juries, but the courts were notoriously biased in favor of the capturing American captain and crew. Prizes were sold for considerable sums, depending on the condition of the ship and value of the cargo. Of course, if a privateer was sunk or captured, the investors lost their entire investment. The crew and owners got all of the money after subtracting expenses.

Privateers, especially those of the Americans, had a devastating effect on British shipping and maritime commerce during the war. Of note, the British House of Lords noted that as of February 1778, Britain had lost a staggering total of 559 vessels to American raiders. According to Maclay, ships of the Continental navy captured 196 English prizes, while the private navy tallied about 600. Maclay further notes that America really won the war by interrupting British maritime commerce, while failing in many land battles against superior English forces. The number of privateers peaked in 1776 at 449; near the end of the war, in 1782, there were only 7 Continental navy warships active. The British navy had only about 24 ships stationed along the North American coast in 1775. The total number of British warships was 270 at the beginning of the Revolution and 478 by the end of the war. Congress commissioned only 50 ships for the Continental navy, most of which were used to raid British commercial vessels.

Privateering was not so popular with one famous Continental naval officer, John Paul Jones. He stated, "The common classes of mankind are actuated by no noble principle than that of self-interest. This and only this determines all adventurers in privateers, the owners as well as those whom they employ."

No doubt the American private navy played a key role in the Revolution. Even though the British navy far outgunned and out-shipped us, we had fisherman-sailors and expert knowledge of the coastline. These advantages proved disastrous for the English.

3

FAMILY BUSINESS

J.P. HAND

To say that many of Cape May's Revolutionary War–era privateers were related by blood or marriage is a gross understatement. The family bonds and business connections of those in the privateer trade from the Cape's relatively small population resulted in a fabric of community as interwoven and strong as the worsted-wool mittens and stockings that the county's women knit for export.

A thorough look at the pedigrees of these men, especially the captains and the owner-investors, reveals an almost unbelievable degree of family connections. Among these patriots we find brothers and brothers-in-law, fathers and sons, uncles and cousins, both first and second. Many of Cape May's privateers were related by blood a few times over, a situation that would continue among the county's population in the centuries that followed and on to the present time. A brief history of the European settlement of the county helps to explain this phenomenon. By 1699, after little more than a decade of permanent settlement, the European population on the Cape consisted of about seventy households. For reasons that will become self-evident, it is important to note that eleven of these, or over one-seventh, had the surname Hand.

By the time of the American Revolution, about eighty years and a couple of generations later, most of these families had intermarried. A slow but steady stream of newcomers, such as the Bennetts, Holmes, Teals and others, married into the early families as well. The majority of these

European families migrated from earlier settlements on eastern and western Long Island, New York. Some Long Island families came directly to Cape May, while others arrived on the Cape by way of East Jersey (North Jersey). According to architectural historian and author Joan Berkey, approximately 70 percent of the earliest settlers at Cape May migrated from the Long Island towns. Others came from settlements on the Delaware River such as Burlington, New Jersey, and Philadelphia, Pennsylvania. A few of the earliest families also arrived from New England or came directly from Old England by way of the Delaware River settlements.

Of particular interest to our story, from East Hampton and Southampton, on the east end of Long Island, came the Hands, Hughes, Leamings, Edwardses and Schellingers. From Western Long Island and/or East Jersey came the Corsons, Stillwells, Willets and Stiteses. The Taylors, Steelmans and others came to Cape May from settlements on the Delaware River. A quick look at the Stillwell and Hand families in particular best illustrates the scope of the family connections between the privateers of Cape May. The Stillwells were among the English families who had settled in Dutch-controlled western Long Island and were baptizing their children in the Dutch Reformed Church of New Amsterdam as early as 1648. Meanwhile, on the opposite end of the island, the patriarch of the Hand family and his many sons were farming and whaling in the English towns of Southampton and East Hampton.

By the 1690s, members of both whaler-yeomen families had settled on the southern tip of Cape May. The two families were joined in 1738 when Captain Nicholas Stillwell Sr. married Sarah Hand, the granddaughter of whaler Thomas Hand. In or about 1748, Captain Stillwell purchased a plantation at the opposite end of the Cape, on the Great Egg Harbor Bay in the Upper Township. Nicholas and Sarah removed to their new plantation and went on to have nine children. This move would change the family dynamics, as many of their children would eventually marry children of families from the northern end of the county. (Two daughters died before reaching adulthood, Amelia, at age fourteen, and Rhuhame, age two.)

Prior to the American Revolution, Nicholas and Sarah's children would marry as follows:

NICHOLAS STILLWELL JR., Cape May militia colonel, sea captain and merchant, married Ruhamah Hand of Middle Township, a distant cousin of his mother and a great-granddaughter of the prominent whaler and judge Shamgar Hand. Nicholas invested in privateer vessels, and some of the prizes taken by Cape May privateers were auctioned off at his plantation, "at Egg Harbour."

ENOCH STILLWELL served as a lieutenant colonel in the Cape May militia and would become one of the most successful of the Cape May–Philadelphia privateer captains (see chapter 11). He married Sarah Savage, the daughter of Joseph Savage and Martha Daniels Savage.

DAVID STILLWELL married Jane Jones and served in the Gloucester County Militia and as a privateer, likely under his brother Enoch. David's father-in-law, Abraham Jones, was himself a veteran of the Revolution.

SOPHIA STILLWELL married Colonel Richard Somers, a prominent merchant and ship owner of Great Egg Harbour, Gloucester County (now Somers Point, Atlantic County). He was a major player in the fight for independence, and his influence was felt from Philadelphia down to Cape May and up the coast to the colonial port of Tuckerton. Colonel Somers procured and delivered armaments, ammunition and other supplies to local militias and privateers throughout the region. He invested in privateer vessels and also served as the banker for many of the privateer captains, owners and crews. Sophia and Richard Somers had five children, including Captain Richard Somers Jr. of Barbary pirate fame.

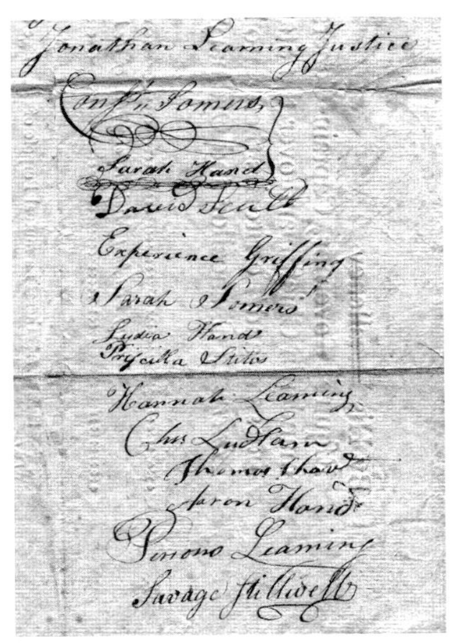

Witness signatures from the wedding of Constant Somers and Sarah Hand, August 1790. *J.P. Hand collection.*

Their eldest son, Constant Somers, married Sarah Hand, the daughter of Jesse Hand Esq. and granddaughter of Aaron Leaming Jr. Esq.

SARAH STILLWELL married Cape May privateer captain Moses Griffing, who was also very successful in his pursuit of British prizes. Griffing, or Griffin as it is sometimes spelled, was a Connecticut native and met his wife shortly before the war began when his vessel put in at Egg Harbor.

HANNAH STILLWELL married Rem Corson, who served in the local militia under his brother-in-law Captain James Willets Jr. and may have served as a privateer crewman under him as well. He was the brother of Captain Darius Corson, another privateer captain from the Cape.

Rebekah Stillwell married Cape May privateer captain James Willets Jr., who was the son of James Willets Sr. and Esther Hand, another granddaughter of Thomas Hand the whaler. Esther was also the aunt of Colonel Elijah Hand and Jonathan Hand Esq. Captain James Willets's brother was Enoch Willets, a Cape May privateer captain who roamed the sea in search of prizes in tandem with his first cousin Captain/Colonel Elijah Hand (see chapter 9). Captain James and Enoch Willets's sister Sarah married Captain Joseph Edwards, another of the Cape May privateers.

> Captain Hand, in the armed boat Enterprize, of Cape May, in company with another boat, commanded by Captain Willets, on the 5th ult. chafed afhore, near Egg-harbour, the refugee boat Old Ranger, mounting feven fwivels and one three pounder, and commanded by one Tryan, with twenty-five men, bound to the capes of Delaware, and up the fame as far as Chriftiana, with orders to take prifoners who they pleafed. They afterwards fell in with and took a fchooner loaded with corn, commanded by one Miller, on a trading voyage from Virginia to New-York; and on the 18th of May they fell in with and took a fchooner laden with lumber, commanded by one Shaw, fuppofed alfo for New-York.

A news report of the exploits of first cousins Elijah Hand and Enoch Willets from Benjamin Franklin's *Pennsylvania Gazette*, June 5, 1782. *Courtesy of the American Antiquarian Society.*

Captain Hope Willets was the cousin of James and Enoch Willets and married Tabitha, the daughter of Colonel John Mackey of the Cape May Militia. The couple's brothers-in-law included privateer captains Darius Corson, who married Martha Mackey, and Joseph Badcock, who married Phoebe Mackey. This Joseph Badcock (the fourth of that name in the county) was the son of Joseph Badcock III and Lydia Hand Badcock. Lydia is believed to be the daughter of whaler Recompence Hand and his wife, Esther. If that is the case, then Captain Joseph Badcock, master of the privateer *Quicktime*, was the first cousin of brothers Captain Enoch Willets and Captain James Willets Jr. as well as that of militia colonel and privateer captain Elijah Hand and his brother Jonathan Hand Esq., both of whom are discussed as follows.

The family connections were just as prevalent among other prominent Cape May families: Colonel Elijah Hand (another grandchild of Thomas Hand the whaler) owned plantations in both Cape May and neighboring Cumberland County. During the Revolution, he rose to the rank of colonel in the Cumberland Militia, and his exploits in that capacity were well known throughout the colonies (see appendix Item 3). He also served as a commander of New Jersey state gunboats and is reported to have captained privateer vessels as well (see appendix Item 1). Captain Elijah Hand is one of the names most often mentioned in the Revolutionary War pension applications of Cape May privateers and soldiers. His son Recompence served in the militia and under him as a privateer crewman.

Elijah's brother Jonathan Hand Esq. served in the last royal legislature and the first state legislature. Their sister Deborah Hand married into the Leaming family and was the aunt of Thomas Leaming III. Leaming may have been the single-most pivotal figure in the story of the Cape May privateers (see appendix Item 4).

Another Hand cousin, Jesse Hand Esq., married Sarah, the daughter of Aaron Leaming Jr. (who was by far the wealthiest man the county has ever produced). Jesse Hand was an important political figure in Cape May County prior to and throughout the war years. He served in the state legislature and was "agent for forfeited estates" during the Revolution. He also co-owned the privateer schooner *Hawk* with Thomas Leaming Jr. and others and owned a saltworks on the Seven Mile Island with his father-in-law, Aaron Leaming Jr., and fellow privateer investor John Holmes.

John Holmes was a recent Irish-Protestant immigrant from Ulster who, with his three brothers, settled in Cape May County just prior to the war. Holmes made a fortune in the relatively brief time he was in America (he died in 1791) and was a pivotal figure in Cape May's privateer trade. He married into the Philadelphia Morris family, while his younger brother, Nathaniel Holmes, married Hannah, the eldest daughter of wealthy tavernkeeper and county sheriff Daniel Hand of the Middle Township (who is not to be confused with his distant cousin Daniel Hand of the Lower Township, who captained the privateer *George*). The young Nathaniel Holmes served as a crewman on privateer vessels owned by Cape May investors, including Thomas Leaming Sr., Jesse Hand, his elder brother John Holmes and others.

Cape Island merchant George Taylor Sr. was involved in the privateer

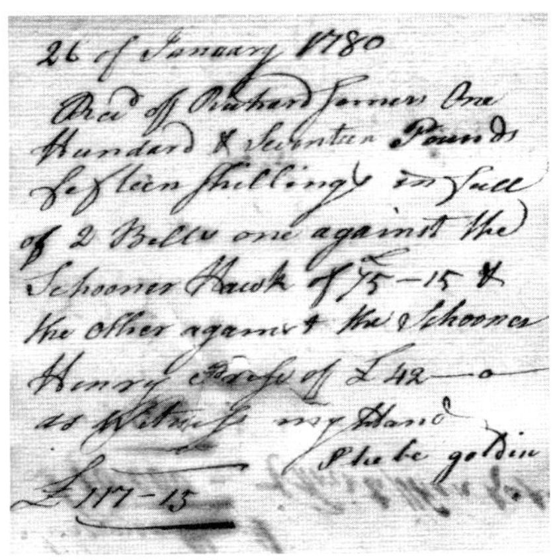

Payment to Phebe Goldin, wife of John Goldin, for shares in prizes of the privateer *Hawk*, from Richard Somers's receipt book. *Private collection.*

trade, as evidenced by this excerpt from his letter of March 24, 1780, to prominent Philadelphia merchant, privateer investor and militia officer Colonel Francis Gurney:

> *I received your letter dated the 11 of this instant march which informed me that you received a bundle of money marked 4933 1/3 of Nathaniel Holmes and I paid to John Holms 5453 1/3 and took his receipt for the same and saw him mark the number on a paper witch he did the same up in so there is a mistake of 520 dollars and it was all large money and easey to be counted and likewise a receipt of paying John Ball Eight thousand six hundred dollars more the whole amounting to 5270 pounds.*

Apparently, younger brother Nathaniel was the mule, ferrying privateer cash between John Holmes at Cape May and Francis Gurney in Philadelphia. What became of the missing currency on the trip to Philadelphia remains a mystery.

George Taylor married Sarah Hand, the daughter of Elias Hand, another descendant of Thomas Hand the whaler. George and Sarah named their son Yelverton most certainly after the famed privateer Captain Yelverton Taylor. This second Yelverton was a thirty-six-year-old widower who married Delia Hand, "both of Cape May," in the Old Swedes Church in Philadelphia on November 22, 1820.

Three of the four earliest families on Cape Island were joined in 1775 when Jane Whilldin bore a son by Captain Humphrey Hughes V. Jane Whilldin was the daughter of wealthy landowner and judge James Whilldin Esq. and his wife, Jane Hand. Local histories and many genealogies claim that the couple married before the birth of their only child, Humphrey Hughes VI. That appears to be a longstanding assumption, as no marriage record has been found to date. This presumption is compounded by the fact that in 1776 the couple was charged in the Cape May court with the crime of fornication (which usually indicates a pregnancy or birth of a child by an unmarried woman). Sometime in late 1778 or 1779, Captain Humphrey Hughes was lost at

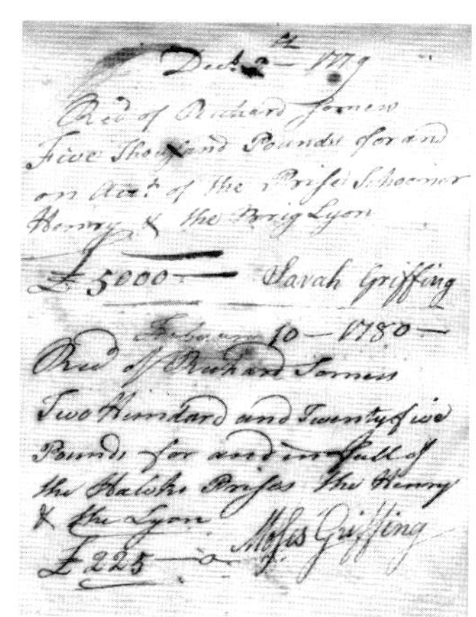

Payments to Sarah Stillwell Griffing and Captain Moses Griffing for shares in prize brig *Lyon* and schooner *Henry* from Richard Somers's receipt book. *Private collection.*

sea with his twenty-five-man crew while serving as master of the privateer sloop *New Comet*. That vessel was owned by Thomas Leaming Jr. and his partners and was believed to have been lost on its first privateer cruise.

The family connections go on and on and may be considered one of the primary forces that led to the success and large scope of this enterprise at Cape May. The benefits of those familial connections can be seen in various ways. Obviously, loyalty would come into play when facing armed combat alongside one's close relatives. The same can be assumed regarding employment opportunities for captains, officers and crew of the privateer vessels.

Among the county's elite, the ability to find the capital to invest in privateer vessels and other wartime enterprises was often made easier with the help of wealthier relatives, as can be seen by this entry in Aaron Leaming's journal dated July 18, 1777:

> *Mr. John Holmes & I having concluded to energize our salt works,* [on Seven Mile Island] *Persons Leaming and he is preparing to set out to buy kettles* [at Reading, Pennsylvania]. *Our aim is to buy 3 tons for him 2 tons for me and 1 ton for Jesse Hand* [Leaming's son-in-law]. *For that purpose I gave Persons £125 to pay in earnest toward the 3 ton for Hand & me, the rest must be paid when the kettles are ready.*

We should note that common salt, while normally one of the least expensive commodities, was extremely valuable during both the American Revolution and the War of 1812 when British warships blockaded most major American ports. This, in turn, led to another war-related industry that stimulated the local economy. During the Revolution, saltworks were set up along the seaside in most of New Jersey's coastal counties and at Cape May, on the Delaware bayside as well. Many of the same merchants who imported munitions and armaments for the war effort also traded in locally produced sea salt. The following entry from Colonel Richard Somers's daybook for his "Old Ferry Store" in Philadelphia offers an example of sea salt being used as currency during the war years:

> *1781*   *Mrs. Leah Holmes*
> *October 27*   *2 gallons of molasses at 3/6 £ - 11 − 0*
> *November 12 Credit*   *Leah Holmes to 14 bushells of salt*

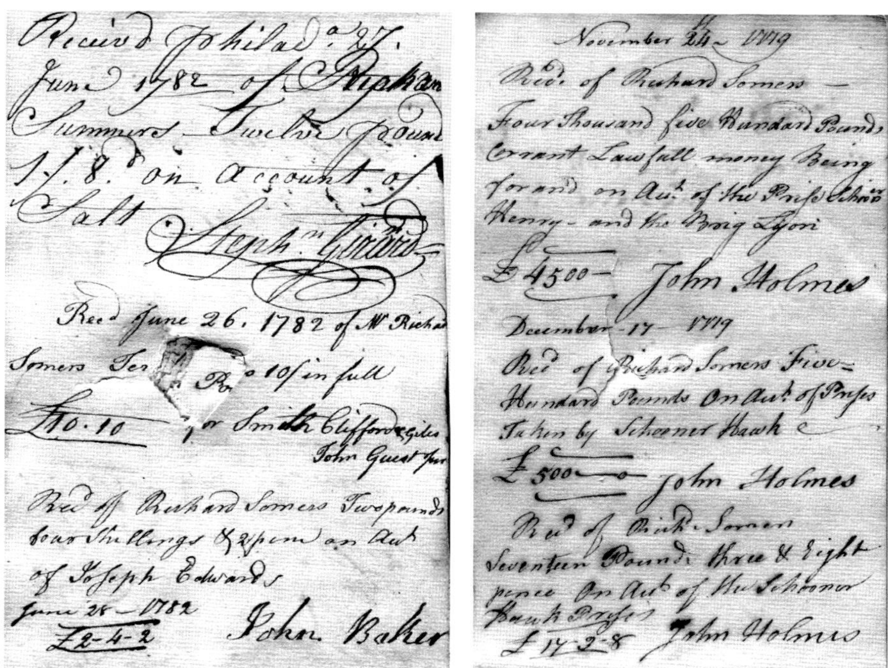

Left: Payment from sea captain turned banker Stephen Girard to Richard Somers for locally produced sea salt, from Richard Somers's receipt book. *Private collection.*

Right: Payments to John Holmes Sr. for his share of prizes taken by the schooner *Hawk*, from Richard Somers's receipt book. *Private collection.*

Leah Holmes operated a tavern in Galeway, Gloucester County (now Galloway Township, Atlantic County) with her husband and former Cape May resident, Captain James Holmes of the Gloucester militia. He was the brother of John Holmes Sr., who co-owned the saltworks mentioned previously. Mrs. Holmes likely took in the fourteen bushels of salt for drinks, victuals and lodging at her tavern from the owners or workmen of the saltworks on nearby Absecon Island. Alternatively, the salt could have come from her brother-in-law's saltworks down in Cape May.

This brief journal entry and others like it help to illustrate how the family ties and business connections of Cape May's privateers extended well beyond the county lines. It should be noted that Captain James Holmes was severely injured at the Battle of Princeton and never fully recovered from his wounds. He died before the war ended in 1783, and when James's elder brother John Holmes died in 1791, he left "all my lands and meadows, lying and being in Galloway and Great Egg Harbour Townships, in Gloucester County, New Jersey" to his nephew and namesake, John Holmes, the only child of James and Leah Holmes.

All of the examples of family and business connections mentioned in this chapter are some of the more obvious ones. Those connections extended outside of Cape May County through marriage and business ventures, tying some of the county's merchant families to others with privateer connections, including the Fishers and Bunners of Philadelphia and the Keens of Salem, New Jersey, and Philadelphia.

4

THE MECHANICS OF PRIVATEERING

THE WRITTEN RECORD

J.P. HAND

WHAT COULD BETTER SHED LIGHT on the mechanics and minute details of the privateering trade at Cape May and its neighboring counties than the ledgers, receipt books and correspondence of the owners of the vessels? Fortunately, many original handwritten volumes on the subject still survive in the collections of various research libraries and in private hands as well.

In particular, the Revolutionary War–era ledgers and receipt books of Thomas Leaming Jr. Esq. and Colonel Richard Somers are a wealth of information regarding the trade. In their own words, the two merchants recorded most every aspect of their privateer activities. In fact, the names of many of Cape May's privateer crewmen and their services would be lost to history if not for the record of payments made to them by Leaming and Somers.

The ledgers contain information such as how the proceeds of the sale of prizes and their cargoes were divided among investors, captains, officers and crew. They also record details such as the different locations where prizes were auctioned off as well as payments made to vendors who provided "stores," including food, drink and other necessary supplies needed during a privateering cruise.

Two particular receipt books, one of Leaming's and one belonging to Somers, list transactions in the order in which they were settled. Pounds, shillings and pence were used to settle almost all of the transactions, but

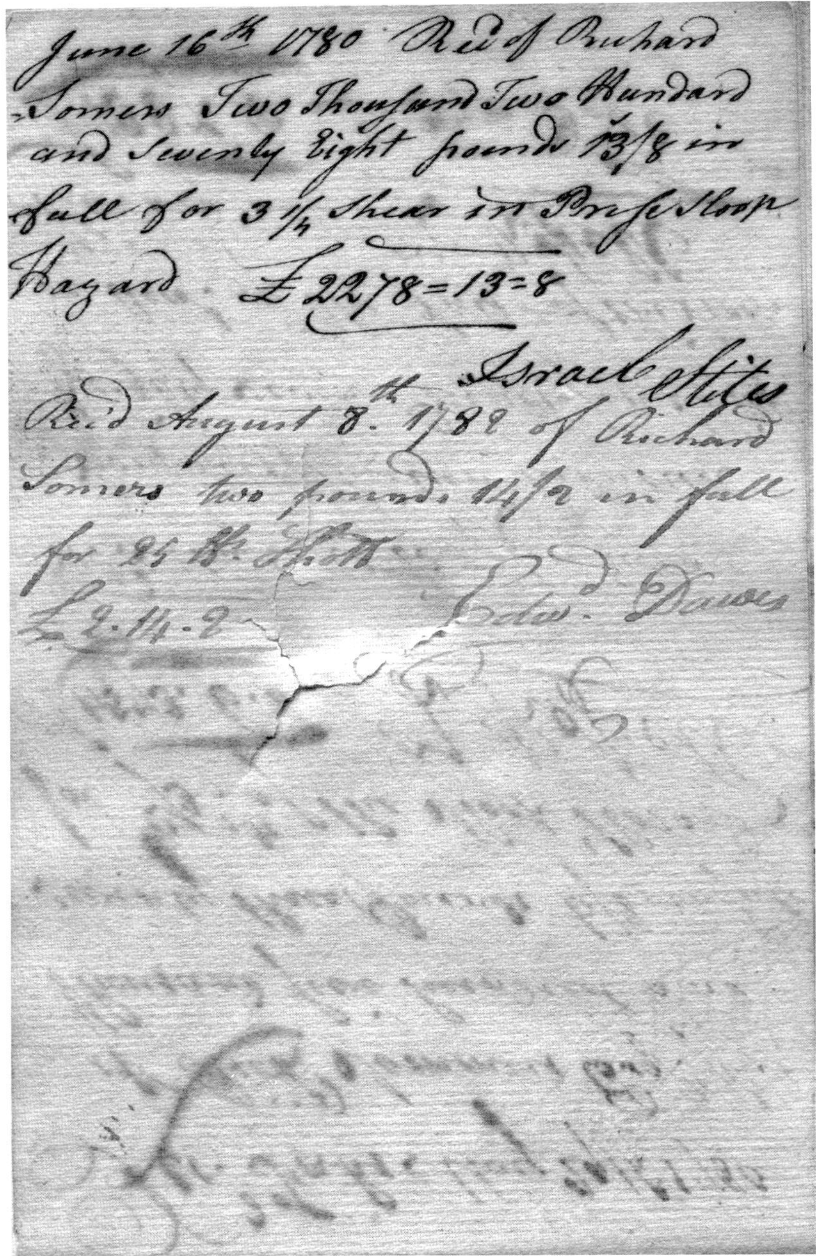

Payment to Israel Stites for 3¼ shares in prize sloop *Hazard*, from Richard Somers's receipt book. *Private collection.*

occasionally the term *dollars* appears. The amounts paid out or received range from a few pounds to payments in the thousands of pounds:

> *Received 12 Nov 1778 of Thomas Leaming Thirty Two pounds 14/ In full for 4 bbls,* [barrels] *bread bought of me for the sloop* New Comet
> *£32:14*   [illegible signature]

> *Recd 13th June 1782 of Mr Richard Somers a role of lead for the use of the Cape May State Boat*
> *John Holmes* [commanded by Colonel Elijah Hand]

> *Receivd 23 Dec 1778 of Tho Leaming Twenty three Pounds 10/ In full for a Mast for the* New Comet
> *£23 = 10*   *Anthony Cuthbert*

> *Receivd 10 Decr 1778 of Tho Leaming five hundred & thirty one pounds in full for Two Casks of Gunpowder*
> *£531*   *by me   Henry Deaberger*

> *Receivd: Dec 18th 1778 of Thom Leaming three hundred & forty four Pounds 15/3 in full for Rope for Schooner* Tryton
> *£344*   *15/3   Johnson & Tittermary*

> *Recd the 23rd Decb 1779 of Richard Somers Two Thousand Pounds in full for a Hogshead of Rum 100 Gallons at £20 per Gal*
> *£2000*   *Daniel Ridge*

> *March 7TH 1780*
> *Recd of Richard Somers Two Thousand Pounds on acct*
> *Of Building the New Ship at Tuckahow* [Tuckahoe]
> *£2000 = 0*   *Abel Lee*

Payments made to ship carpenters and other tradesmen for repairs to privateer vessels were recorded in detail. Few, if any vessels could sail up or down the Delaware Bay and River without the aid of an experienced pilot due to the constantly changing channels and shoals. The fees paid to members of that exclusive fraternity were recorded as well:

Received 8 Dec 1778 of Thos Leaming. Seven pounds 17/6 for work
done on board, the Happy Return
Jas Leach   Master
£7 17/6   Recd. By me Wm Thomson

Recd Dec 16 1778 of Thomas Leaming Twenty Six Pounds in full for
Carpenter Work on Schooner Mars
£26 7   Wm Coats

Received 14 Nov 1778 of Thos Leaming Seven pounds 5/6 for cleaning
& repairing 4 Muskits for the Sloop Comet
£7 5/6   George Connel

Febuary 17 1780 Recd of Richard Somers One Hundred & Fifty pounds
for and on acct of Brown Benet [Bennet] *Piloting Brig* Lyon
£150   Enoch Stillwell

Received 28 Nov. 1778 of Tho Leaming Thirty Nine pounds 7/6 in full
for Poiloting the Sloop Comet *as pr*
Captn Hughes Orders
£39 7/6   Nathan Church

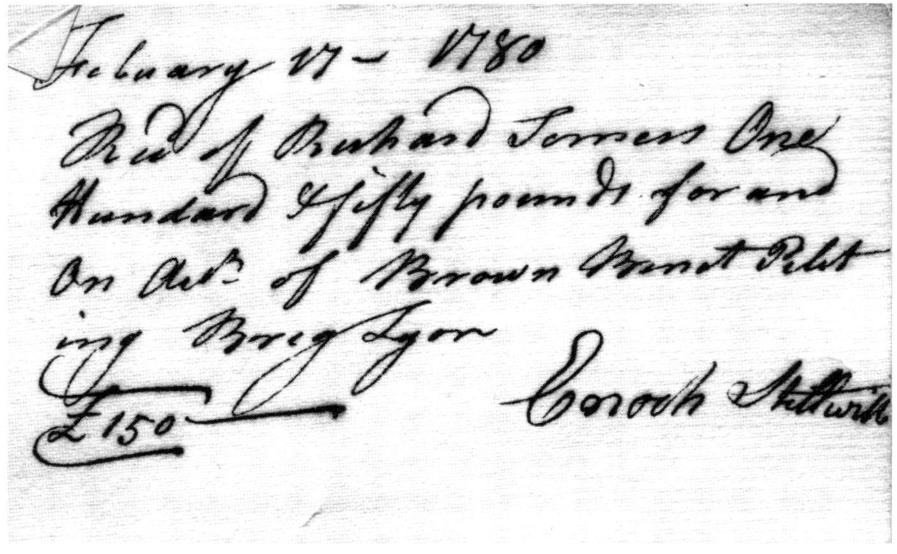

Payment to pilot Brown Bennet for piloting the prize brig *Lyon*, from Richard Somers's receipt book. *Private collection.*

Right: Payment to Cape May residents John Cresse and his wife for the care of Captain Childs, master of the captured British brig *Lyon*. Also, a receipt for a hogshead of rum from the *Lyon*, from Richard Somers's receipt book. *Private collection.*

Below: Most of the prizes captured by the privateers of Cape May were auctioned off at locations away from the coast and out of the reach of large British warships. This auction was held at the house of Captain James Willets on the banks of the Tuckahoe River, *Pennsylvania Packet*, August 24, 1782. *Courtesy of the American Antiquarian Society.*

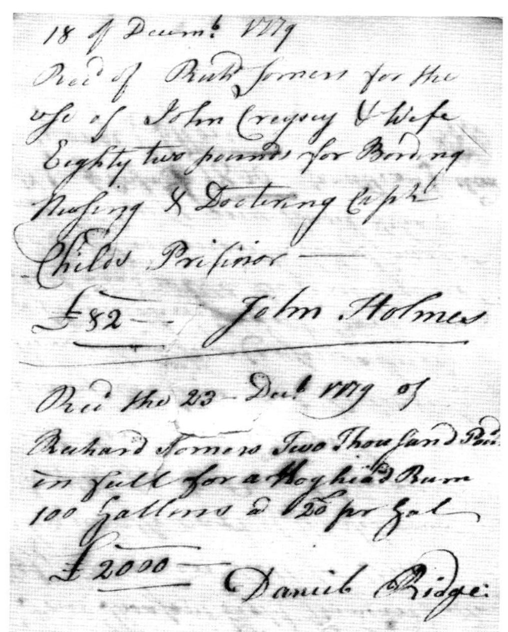

Will be Sold on Wednesday the 28th of this instant, at the house of James Willet, on Cape May, two armed BOATS, named the True Blue and Gibraltar, with their guns and appurtenances. The Vendue to begin at 10 o'clock in the morning.

By order of the Judge of the admiralty, August 20, 1782.   JAMES M'COMB, Marshal.

Privateering was to a large degree a business, but a dangerous one at that. The owners of privateer vessels appeared to have been loyal to their crews; crewmen were awarded extra prize money for being wounded, and quite a few accounts were settled after a crew member was deceased. The following entries reveal the more personal and sometimes tragic side of the trade:

Recd July 7, 1780 of Thomas Leaming Jr. Three Hundred Dollars being the crew of the schooner Addition *Share of Bounty allowed me for being wounded on board her while she was cruising as a Privateer in 1778*

£112 "10 "0   John Snider alias John Taylor
[n.b. conversion of dollars into pounds]

18 of Decemb 1779 Recd of Richard Somers for the use of John Creysey
[Cresse] *& wife*
Eighty two pounds for Bording Nursing & Doctoring Capt Childs Prisoner
[Master of the prize brig, Lyon]
£82   John Holmes

By Virtue of Direction from Humphrey Hughes to settle all his Prize Accounts I have this Day settled with Thomas Leaming jr the Accounts of sd. Humphrey Hughes which is include his Share of the Prize Sloops Lark & Polly & their Respective Cargos & have Recd the Sum of Two Hundred & Ninety Eight Pounds 14 / 6/3/4 the Ball. Of said accounts this 15ᵗʰ Day of Feb 1781 David Bowen
£298 - 14 - 6¾
[n.b. Captain Humphrey Hughes and his twenty-five-man crew were lost at sea prior to this disbursement.]

Recd May 1ˢᵗ 1781 of Thomas Leaming thirty pounds 7½ a Ball [balance] *of Prize Money due my brother John Pancake from Prize Brig. Recovery & Cargo who is supposed to be lost at sea.*
Phillip Pancake

Payments listed in the receipt books reflect the stature or value of any given crew member. Young or inexperienced crewmen received relatively small shares of prize money in comparison to the amounts paid to experienced crewmen and officers. It appears to have been a common practice for privateer crewmen to sell their shares to others for cash instead of waiting for future payment:

Recd Dec 10ᵗʰ 1779 of Thomas Leaming jr. Sixteen Pounds 13/8 in full for my share of Schooner Phenix [Phoenix] *& Cargo*
£16 18/8   Jeremiah Marshall

Recd Feb 10 1780 of Thomas Leaming jr. thirty pounds 8/
For Reubin Bates Half Share of Prize Money in Brig Recovery
£30 8/   Moses Griffing

Rec March 10th 1780 of Thomas Leaming jr. Twenty Pounds 15/1 the Ball of Prize Money due me for my
one share of Prize Brig Recovery *& Cargo*
£20 15/1   Nath Holmes

Recd Jun 28th 1780 of Thomas Leaming jr. One Hundred & Twenty One Pounds 12/2 in full of John Stites
two shares of Brig Recovery *& Cargo as an officer on board the Sch.*
Addition *Capn Griffing which Shares he sold me*
£121 12/2   B Randolph

Recd April 7th 1780 of Thomas Leaming Jr. Six Pounds 13/0 ¼ in full of Ball of Acct respecting Prize Money due me as one of the Crew of Sloop Comet
Capn. Yelverton Taylor
£6 13/0 ¼   Matthias Taylor

Recd Febr 10th 1780 of Thomas Leaming jr. Sixty Pounds 15/1 for John Scotts Share of Prize Money in Brig Recovery *also Ninety Eight Pounds 8/2 a Ball in John Badcocks 2 shares of Prize Money of sd. Brig, also One Hundred and Ninety three Pounds 13/4 Ball in William Treens Share of Prize Money in sd. Brig also Eight Pounds 13/1 Ball in John Aarons one Share of Prize Money in said Brig* Recovery
£362 0/8   James Willets

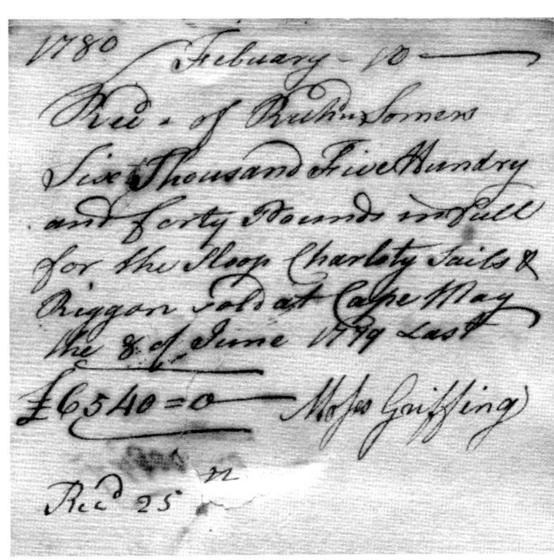

Payment to Captain Moses Griffing for prize sloop *Charloty*, from Richard Somers's receipt book. *Private collection.*

The entries in Thomas Leaming's receipt book mostly concern payments made to crewmen and vendors on behalf of himself and his partners. It appears that Colonel Richard Somers made the large payments due to the Cape May captains and investors.

The following entries from Somers's receipt book show that the real money went to those captains, owners and other investors. Most of the transactions listed below are from the sale of two prizes, the British brig *Lyon* and the schooner *Henry*, captured by Captain Enoch Stillwell in the privateer schooner *Hawk* (ten guns, fifty men):

November 20th 1779
Recd of Richard Somers this day Twenty Thousand Seven Hundred &
Twenty Nine Pounds five shillings
on Acct. of Prize money in the Schooner Henry *& The Brig* Lyon.
£20729 /5   Enoch Stillwell

Decb 6 1779
Recd of Richard Somers Five Thousand Pounds on Acct of the Prize Brig
Lyon *& the Schooner* Henry
£5000   Enoch Stillwell

November 25 1779
Recd of Richard Somers Four Thousand Pounds on Acct of Prize money
in the Schooner Henry *& the Brig* Lyon
£4000   William Treen

November 24th 1779
Recd of Richard Somers Four Thousand five Hundred Pounds current
lawful money Being for and on Acct.
of the Prize Schooner Henry *and the Brig* Lyon
£4500   John Holmes

Dec 5th 1779
Recd of Richard Somers Five Thousand Pounds for and on Acct of the
Prize Schooner Henry *& the Brig* Lyon
£5000   Sarah Griffing [wife of Captain Moses Griffing and sister of Captain Enoch Stillwell]

February 10 1780
Recd of Richard Somers Two Hundred and Twenty five Pounds for and in
full of the Hawks *Prizes The*
Henry *&* The Lyon
£225 Moses Griffing

Dec 4 1779
Recd of Richard Somers Agt [Agent] *for the Schooner* Hawk *Five*
Thousand four Hundred and Eighteen Pounds fifteen Shillings for the use
of John Bray Being the Equal Two and thirteth part of the Neat [net]
Proceeds of the Prize Brig Lyon *which said 32nd part was Purchased of*
Robert Snell by J Bray
£5418 15   Jos Potts

[n.b. Militia officer and privateer captain Robert Snell sold John Bray his 1/32nd share of the net proceeds of the brig Lyon. The thirty-two shares of that one valuable prize amounted to a total net value of over £173,000.]

1780 Febuary 10
Recd of Richard Somers Six Thousand five Hundred and Forty Pounds
in full for the Sloop Charloty *Sails & Riggon* [Rigging] *Sold at Cape*
May the 8th of June las
£6540   Moses Griffing

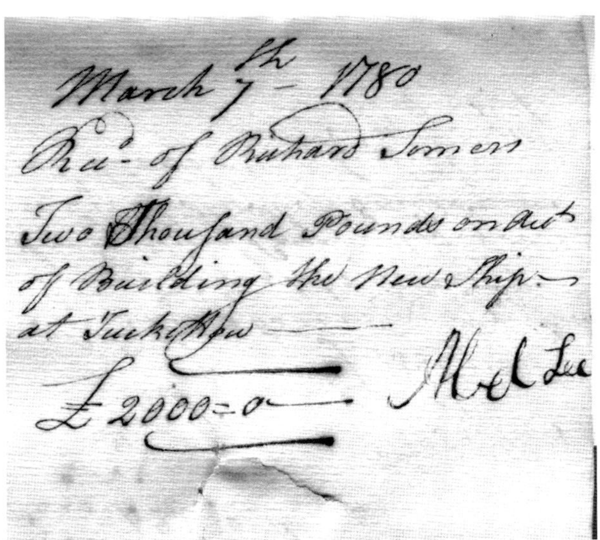

Payment toward the building of a privateer vessel at Tuckahoe, Cape May County, by shipbuilder Abel Lee, from Richard Somers's receipt book. *Private collection.*

March 1ˢᵗ 1780
Recd of Richard Somers for the use of Jesse Hand One Hundred and Sixty
two pounds Sixteen Shillings and five pence on Acct. of schooner Hawk
Prizes
£162 16/5   John Holmes

June 16ᵗʰ 1780
Recd of Richard Somers Two Thousand Two Hundred and Seventy Eight
Pounds 13/8 in full for 3¼
Shear [share] *in Prize Sloop* Hazard
£2278 13/8   Israel Stites

January 13ᵗʰ 1781
Recd of Richard Somers Four Thousand five Hundred Pounds ___ of all
for One Sixteenth part of the Schooner G [Governor] Livingston *now*
lying at Mr J. Carsons Wharf
£4500   James Willets

OUTFITTING THE PRIVATEER SCHOONER *HAWK*

Just how would a group of private investors go about acquiring armaments for a privateer vessel in the late eighteenth century? Fortunately for modern historians, contemporary newspaper accounts and surviving correspondence of Colonel Richard Somers and others describe that process in detail for the Cape May "owned and operated" privateer schooner *Hawk*. Part of that story begins with a legal notice that appeared in the *New-Jersey Gazette* on June 2, 1779:

TO BE SOLD by way of public vendue, at the house of Col. Nicholas
Stillwill, on Cape-May, on Monday the 7ᵗʰ day of June, as she now lies
stranded on Peck's Beach,
The hull of the letter of marque brig DELIGHT.
And at the same time and place will be sold the cargo of said brig,
consisting of eighty puncheons of good West-India rum, about one ton
of gunpowder, a number of small arms, and two or three tons of cannon
ball; together with the great guns, cables, anchors, sails, rigging, and
furniture of said brig

By order of the Court of Admiralty,
JOS. POTTS, Marshal.
New-Jersey, May, 27, 1779

At some point before May 27, 1779, the British or Tory privateer *Delight* had run aground on Peck's Beach (Ocean City, New Jersey) and had been captured and claimed by the local militia. The sale of the prize and its cargo was to be held at the plantation of Cape May militia colonel Nicholas Stillwell Jr., whose brother Enoch Stillwell was master of the *Hawk*.

It appears that five of the primary owners of the *Hawk* converged at the auction site and coordinated their purchases toward arming and outfitting the vessel. To reach the venue site, Richard Somers either crossed the Great Egg Harbor Bay or traveled from Philadelphia, where he kept a home and owned several businesses. Likewise, Thomas Leaming Jr. was living in Philadelphia but owned multiple plantations back home in Cape May County. Wealthy merchant and militia captain Thomas Sinnickson either traveled across West Jersey on poor roads or traveled by vessel from his home in the town of Salem, Salem County. Jesse Hand and captain/owner Enoch Stillwell were both living in Middle Township, Cape May County, at the time and would have had a relatively short journey of fifteen to twenty miles up the Seaside Road to the "vendue." In the case of Enoch Stillwell, the venue was the Stillwell home plantation where he had been born and raised.

While other bidders may have purchased most of the cargo of rum, various owners of the *Hawk* snapped up much of the armaments, military stores, small arms and miscellaneous gear. In a letter/invoice addressed to "Colonel Richard Summers at Great Egg Harbour" from Cape May's Jesse Hand dated July 14, 1779, Hand records in detail what he and some of his partners purchased on June 7 at Nicholas Stillwell's auction:

> *Sir*
>
> *Mr Sinexson* [Captain Thomas Sinnickson] *Requested me to Draw out the Bills which the owners of the Schooner had purchased for her use and send them to you as soon as possible; He Requested that I would mention to you that Capt Stocker and Marshal had Each one Equal share of all the Ball purchased by him Except those purchased at Youngs and that the Schooner Ought to have Credit for so Much out of bill, he Likewise Requested me to Mention to you that there was a division Made by Leaming and Stocker of the Articles Leaming Purchased at Vendue and Requests that you would Mention it to Leaming to know whether we had for the use of*

*the Schooner the full amount of Articles Mentioned in his bills, I Remain
Sir with Respect your Friend and Very Humble Servant
Mr Richard Sumers Jesse Hand*

Brig Delight *vendue*

Majer [Enoch] *Stillwell*	£3102 – 15
Mr Thom Leaming	58 – 10
Mr [Thom] *Sinnskon*	1835 – 1
Mr [Richard] *Somers*	349 –
Mr [Jesse] *Hand*	224 –

£6069 = 6

Jesse Hand's letter includes accounting for the purchases of all five owners mentioned, with Thomas Leaming and Captain Stillwell's listed below:

Major Enoc Stillwill *June 7, 1779*

Bt [bought] *at Vendue Brig* Delight

2 Carriage Guns	£2055 –
5 Gun Carriages	£125 –
8 Empty Hogsheads	£25 –
1 Cask and Meat	£6 – 5
1 Lot of Roaps	£56 –
1 Ditto	£16
1 Ditto	£96 –
1 Ditto	£84
1 Ditto	£49
1 Ditto	£58
1 Bag Musket Ball	£44 – 10
1 Ditto	£82 –
1 Cag [Keg] *Tallow*	£71
1 Sail	£292
1 Sail	£59

£3102 – 15

Mr Thomas Leaming Junr.   June 7 1779
Bot at Vendue Brig Delight

1 Gun	*£5 –*
1 Blunderbuss	*11 – 10*
1 Do [ditto]	*15 – 10*
1 Do	*12 – 10*
1 Gun	*6 – 10*
1 Pair Pistols	*13 – 10*
1 Ditto	*20 –*
1 Ditto	*23 –*
1 Ditto	*26 – 10*
1 Pistol	*18 –*
1 Gun	*15 –*
1 Ditto	*14 – 10*
1 Ditto	*14 – 10*
1 Cutlass	*2 – 10*
1 Bick Iron [small anvil]	*11 –*
1 Camboos [caboose, cookroom or galley]	*180 –*
1 Blunderbuss	*24 –*
1 Chest	*30 –*
1 Cag and Iron	*54 –*

£497 – 10
1 Barrel Beef   *61*

£558 – 10

Another document from the same collection rounds out the list of owners of the privateer schooner *Hawk* and accounts for eight more of the vessel's ten cannons. Thomas Leaming Jr.'s firm, Bunner, Murre & Company, apparently penned the invoice marked "Acct. Hawk with Several Owners." Additional owners are listed, including several privateer captains of Cape May as well as two Gloucester County militia officers:

Owners of the Schooner Hawk   *Det* [Debtor]
1779
June 7ᵗʰ Bought at Vendue Brig Delight   *£6069 – 6*
Bought at vendue Sloop Charloty

To 7 New Sails	*5000 –*
To a Lot of Riggon [rigging]	*750 –*
To Thomas Sinnukson Bill Provisions	*2186 –*
To Richard Somers Bill	*4199 – 7 – 10*
To Joseph Ball Bill for 6 guns	*4500*
To Commissions at 5 percent	*1135 – 4*
To Bunner Murre & C. Bill	*3903 – 5 – 5*

Total	*£27743 – 3 – 3*

To 1 pare four Pounders Lent to Schooner
To 1 cable and Anchor Lent   Do
To 1 pump Lent   Do

Each mans proportion of Outfits of Schooner Hawk

To Bunner Murre & Co – 38 – 96 [shares]	*£10981 – 13*
To Thom. Sinnukson – 13 – Ditto	*3756 – 17*
To R Somers 15	*4334 – 17 – 6*
To Mager Stillwill [Enoch] *6*	*1733 – 19*
To Jesse Hand Esq 6	*1733 – 19*
To Capt Christ. Rape 6	*1733 – 19*
To Capt [James Jr.] *Willits 3*	*866 – 19 – 6*
To Willm Treen 3	*866 – 19 – 6*
To Doc[tor] *Rennard 3*	*866 – 19 – 6*
To Capt [Robert] *Snell 3*	*866 – 19 – 6*

	£27743 = 3 = 3

The surviving documents relating to the owners of the *Hawk* reveal the extraordinary amount of behind-the-scenes planning and teamwork required to outfit and man just one privateer vessel, particularly a vessel with ten guns and a fifty-man crew. The financial burden alone might cause a potential investor to hesitate to enter the business. As it was, the owners of the *Hawk* seem to have fared well. The initial outfitting, which totaled £27,743, returned the staggering sum of £173,000 with the capture of the prize brig *Lyon* alone. Even allowing for the eventual capture of the *Hawk* by the British (possibly within a year) and the resulting losses incurred, the initial investment appears to have been money well spent.

Of course, many similar scenarios resulted in vessels captured by the enemy or lost at sea without even recouping the owners' initial investment. The loss of Cape May's own Captain Humphrey Hughes and the privateer schooner *New Comet* is a tragic example of the dangers that could befall a privateer. The *New Comet* was owned by many of the same men who invested in the *Hawk*, and the vessel and crew disappeared without a trace while on a privateering cruise.

5

THE WIEDERHOLDT AFFAIR

D.P. STITES

A REMARKABLE SERIES OF EVENTS connects a group of Hessian mercenaries who fought for the British with two privateers closely related to Cape May. Captain Andreas Wiederholdt, a Hessian soldier, and a good number of his regiment were captured under unusually fortuitous circumstances by two New Jersey–Pennsylvania privateers. One privateer ship, *Comet*, was captained by Stephen Decatur Sr. and the other, *Mars*, by Yelverton Taylor. Although Taylor was probably born in Pennsylvania, he had close ties to Cape May, as did Decatur. Stephen Decatur was the father of the famous War of 1812 naval officer Stephen Decatur Jr. The narration of the events leading up to and including the capture of Wiederholdt and his British troop ship, *Triton*, in September 1779 is derived from the diary of Captain Wiederholdt, written originally in German. Because of the vivid historical picture it presents, significant excerpts are reprinted here, as translated by the author.

Who were the so-called Hessians? King George III augmented the British troops who were sent to fight against the Rebels with a large number of mercenaries from several German principalities, including:

Brunswick	5,723 soldiers
Hesse-Cassel	16,992 soldiers
Hesse-Hanau	2,422 soldiers
Anspach-Bayreuth	2,353 soldiers

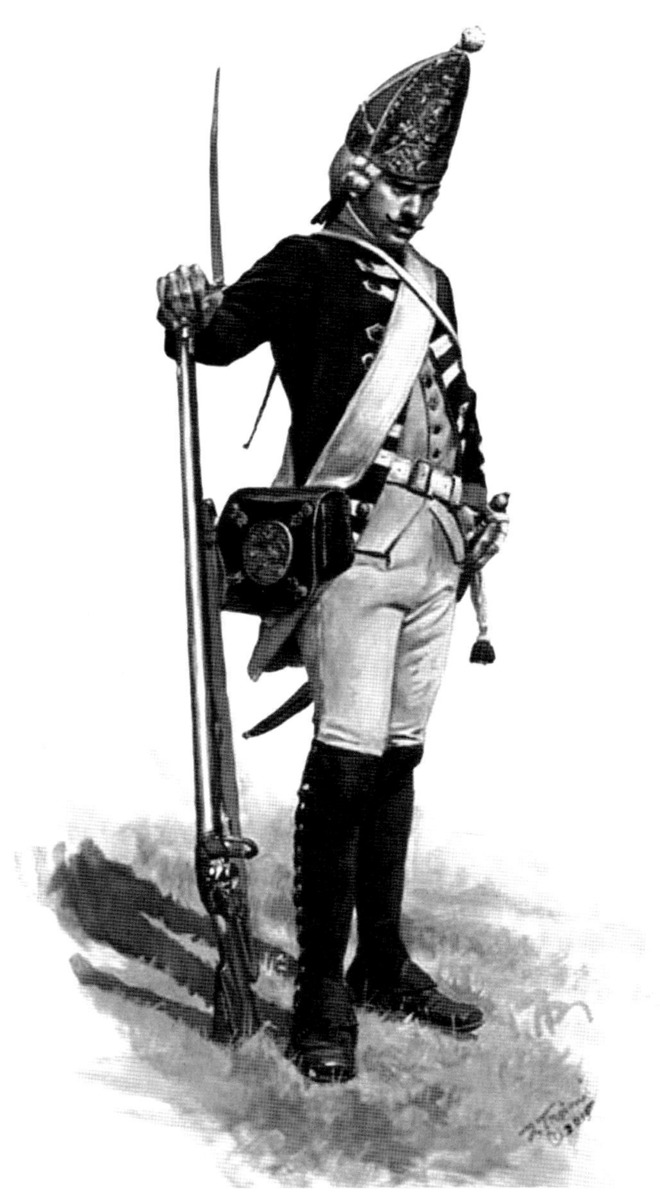

Hessian soldier. *Dan Stites collection*.

Waldeck	1,225 soldiers
Ahnalt-Zerbst	1,152 soldiers
Total	29,867 men

Many of these men did not return to Germany. Lowell estimates that about 12,500 were killed, died of illness or accident or deserted. Many others remained and eventually became Americans. The total British-German forces totaled about 50,000, so a significant part was made up of these paid warriors from Germany.

Andreas Wiederholdt is first mentioned as a German lieutenant at the Battle of New York as a member of the Von Knyphausen regiment of Hessians. In November 1776, Wiederholdt played an import role in the capture of Fort Washington, later named Fot Knyphausen, in New York City. Lieutenant General Wilhelm von Knyphausen was in charge of the Second Division of Hessians and was the second in command of the expeditionary German forces under General Leopold Philip de Heister. Wiederholdt's regiment was named for General von Knyphausen and was commanded by Colonel Johann Rall, who was later killed at the Battle of Trenton.

Washington's army was badly defeated in New York and gradually retreated to New Jersey. The troops crossed the Delaware into Pennsylvania on December 8, 1776. Colonel Rall's brigade was made up of three regiments of Hessians: von Lossberg, von Knyphausen and Rall. The von Knyphausen regiment quartered near Trenton. On the fateful night of December 24, 1776, Wiederholdt, joined by Hessian colleagues, served as a picket near the town of Pennington, New Jersey. That night, Washington's ragtag army of 2,400 crossed the Delaware into New Jersey. Due primarily to Colonel Rall's foolish underestimation of the American forces and resolve, the Hessians were defeated by Washington's army over the course of the next few days. The victories at Trenton and later Princeton were major turning points in favor of the American Rebels. Rall was mortally wounded at the Battle of Trenton and buried in an unmarked grave in Trenton. Most of the Hessians were captured and marched across the Delaware to Pennsylvania. Wiederholdt and seventeen of his men were initially under the surveillance of the American general Lord Stirling.

Along with other captured Hessian officers, Wiederholdt was initially quartered in Newton, Bucks County, Pennsylvania, the location of Washington's headquarters. In those days, captured officers were often dined by their captors in what seems today as an unusually polite gesture. What follows is a verbatim translation of Andreas Wiederholdt's meeting with and impressions of General George Washington:

December 28, 1776
I dined as mentioned earlier with several officers and General Washington. He did me the honor to converse with me about the unfortunate affair (Trenton and Princeton). I gave him my frank opinion that our situation had been very unfavorable which resulted in our falling into his hands. He asked me how our situation could have had a better outcome. I detailed several mistakes and told him how I would have handled things and escaped with honor. He not only praised this explanation but elegized about my alertness and defense with my men on the picket line the morning of the attack.

General Washington is a polite and refined man. He appears reserved and polite, seldom speaks and has a crafty physiognomy. He is not tall but neither short, best described as average in height and waistline. He resembles Captain von Bisenrod of the von Knyphausen regiment. He gave me permission to go to Trenton to look for my writings there.

In January 1777, Wiederholdt and his captured colleagues embarked on a march that eventually took them south into Virginia as far as Dumfries, where they spent most of the winter in captivity. They did not languish in prisons but were guarded by American militia and lived in farmhouses or inns. Wiederholdt makes many references to all the varied flora and fauna of America of the late eighteenth century. Eventually, he and his men made their way back north through the Shenandoah Valley to Winchester, Virginia, and eventually, in December 1777, to Fredericksburg, which he described "as the best and most pleasant place I have seen in America." During his stay, he fell in love with an American girl. The captives were marched farther across the Potomac River in Maryland, where they encamped at Hanover.

In April 1778, Wiederholdt returned to Philadelphia, where he and other Hessians were exchanged for American prisoners, presumably including some of those from prison ships in Wallabout Bay, New York. His comments about the large American city were as follows:

Philadelphia is a large and beautiful place, which is well located for trade, but not as well as New York, because all the products of the province from the inner parts must be brought in wagons.…The Delaware is navigable for some distance inland. The Schuylkill can be travelled by boats for a short distance above Philadelphia because six or eight miles above Philadelphia a major waterfall is to be found therein. This great city is an assembly point for all religions and nations, and therefore a mish-mash of men of all sects and beliefs, no less of scoundrels, and I believe that it is in no way inferior to the cities of Sodom and Gomorrah concerning all depravities.

Back in British hands, the Hessians then marched on to Cooper's Ferry in Camden, New Jersey, where they crossed the Delaware. It was at this time in June 1778 that General Clinton and the British evacuated Philadelphia for fear of a French invasion and headed back to New York. The Hessians marched across New Jersey through Haddonfield, Morristown and Mount Holly with the retreating British. Then they traveled on to Monmouth and eventually to Sandy Hook, New Jersey. The Germans then ended up in British-occupied New York City and spent the winter of 1779 camped on Staten Island.

The fateful events that led to Wiederholdt's recapture began on September 8, 1779, when his regiment disembarked from Sandy Hook, New Jersey, for what at that time was an undisclosed destination. The von Knyphausen and von Lossberg regiments were quartered in three transport vessels, *Triton, Molly* and *Archer.* Wiederholdt and his Hessian colleagues were on the *Triton,* a two-masted brigantine carrying ten cannons. The ship was in rather miserable condition; officers had to sleep on deck, and the sailors' hammocks fell apart after a few days. Privies were in short supply, and vinegar—an essential cleaning solution and antiscorbutic—was totally missing. There were only seven crew members out of what should have been a full complement of eighteen.

On the way out of New York Harbor, it was apparent that the shorthanded *Triton* could not keep up with the other ships in the small convoy. On September 10, separated from the fleet and lacking specific orders, the captain returned to Sandy Hook. This port was the principal harbor in the New York vicinity for the British fleet during the Revolution. Upon the Hessians' return, they encountered other ships, which they initially identified as enemy vessels. Guns were prepared for a battle, but they were found to be in nearly unusable condition. However, the ships turned out to be British, and the *Triton* sailed into port at Sandy Hook again.

On September 11, an agent for the fleet came aboard the *Triton* and gave orders to sail to Quebec. He brought two totally inexperienced boys with him to augment the crew. They set sail and were rapidly blown off course in a strong gale, south to 39 degrees, 30 minutes latitude, which is at

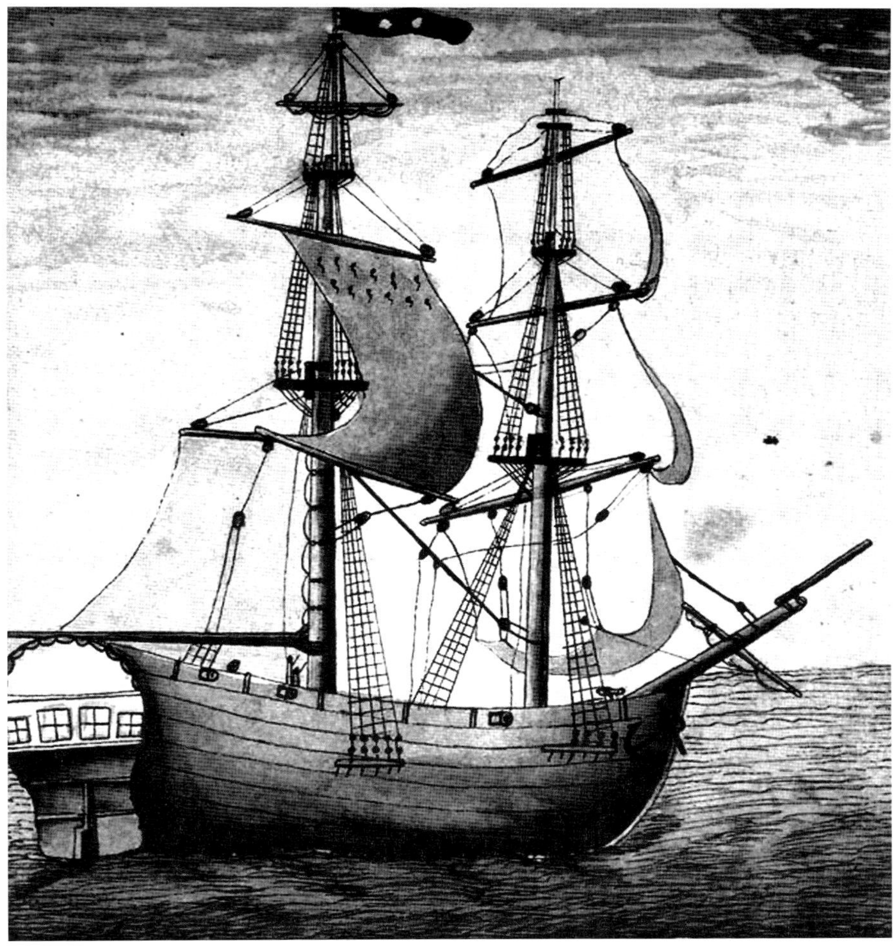

Triton before the storm. *University of Pennsylvania Library.*

the level of Long Beach, New Jersey, over one hundred miles south of their embarkation point. By September 13, the wind picked up to gale force from the northeast, and the *Triton* was in the grips of a severe northeaster with hurricane-force winds.

The following is a translation of Wiederholdt's account of the terrifying events of the next few days in the teeth of the storm:

15 September: The waves swirled up like frightful mountains and the ship was on the verge of being swallowed up by the sea. One minute we were at the peak of such a horrible wave and then driven down into the depths of its trough where the sky was invisible and we appeared to be buried. No ship from the fleet was visible and what terrified us even more was that night had fallen. One could not see one's hand before one's face. It rained and hailed incessantly. The wind roared frightfully and the waves raged amazingly causing such a din and roar that it was extremely fearsome and shattering to hear. At 9:00 the mainmast snapped at the lowest yardarm and fell with a crash into the sea. It was fortunate that several of our officers brought their axes along. There was neither a ship's carpenter aboard nor one axe on the ship otherwise to be had. All aboard the ship screamed, "Axes, axes."

One needed to chop away the rigging and the mast which was now hanging overboard to avoid having the ship pulled under and capsizing. We hadn't finished doing all this when with even a louder crack the foremast broke right over the deck of the ship. We hastened to clear the decks with increased vigor and the ship totally lost her heading into the wind. The angry waves pushed us to and fro with even more force so that the ship would list completely on her side and take in water. These gruesome waves battered us from all sides and even in the stern over the captain's cabin. We had to nail shutters over the glass window panes in his cabin. As we were doing this a wave struck us with such force that the captain was thrown by a stream of water all the way across his cabin floor. In all the to and fro from forceful motion of the boat the guns ripped loose from their moorings and rolled back and forth across the main deck. They crashed into the galley and knocked a huge kettle loose. The four cannons now loose broke through the gunwale and crashed into the sea. The fifth cannon also broke loose and fell through the hatchway into the bilge of the ship right past where the soldiers were on the lower deck. The cannon came to rest wedged between two water barrels and we lashed it to them with rope. The sixth cannon slid back and forth until it crashed into the ship's wheel and splintered it to bits. The sailors refused to try and secure the rolling cannon and returned to their bunks being afraid to lose an arm or a leg in stopping it. All our possessions lay strewn around the ship amidst the sounds of sighing, shining and occasional praying. All felt that the last moments of their lives had come.

In this saddened state I crawled around below sick with fear and spoke to the men trying to raise their spirits. God who had brought us into this danger was also the powerful God who will deliver us if we can get the cannon overboard and work the pumps to free the ship of water and let her then float. Daybreak will come and heaven will send us help by clearing the weather or by sending a ship to our aid. My speech was initially without effect. The men were stubborn and some answered that they were too sick and could not hope. I will tell you that they all very well knew that I was sick with paroxysms of fever for more than four weeks and very ill when I boarded the ship. But out of concern for them and in our desperate situation, I tried to find a way to help. I did not doubt that some of them had more strength than I and cared enough to follow my lead. I wished to remain on deck and share their fate since I had faith that both we and the ship would survive. But no one seemed to respond until I asked if there was no junior officer who was healthy and whether a single Hessian soldier had the courage to help and follow me? So Sgt. Hildebrand, Corporals Orstadt and Kustner came forward followed by another fifteen to twenty men. Ok, I said, let's get the last cannon loose and free it up so we can heave it into the water. After several attempts with great danger to life and limb we managed to get it overboard. One fusilier sustained two broken arms and I crushed a small finger on my left hand. We then manned the pumps and four men continuously worked them lashed to the stump of the mast. They had to switch off every six to eight minutes because they could not stand, but had to kneel to work the pumps.

The pumping lasted until three or four in the morning when they finally broke and were no longer serviceable. Due to darkness we could not repair them. So we fixed a large bucket to a rope and bailed by hand until the long awaited morning broke and we could begin to fix the pumps. Now a marvelous event occurred that must be told.

During the severe motion of the ship one of Col. Heymels fusiliers called Eckhard was thrown overboard. He disappeared rapidly but somehow managed to just barely cling to the side of the ship. He cried for help but went unheard and was missed by the crew. He was hanging on to the ship and called repeatedly for help. Then a huge wave came and washed him right back onto the deck saving the poor fellow for long and healthy life. Truly a wonderful rescue! Meanwhile the captain and the helmsman and the other crewmen walked around the ship with lanterns attempting to free some of the ships boats. I inquired whether they wanted to save themselves and questioned them about their action. "Oh nothing, I only see if they are fast enough." I didn't trust him and demanded he hand me the lantern for a moment. I passed them on to my man and took the captain by the arm and led him away behind his cabin. "I know exactly what you intend. You are fixing the boats to escape and leave us stranded on this ruined ship. We will surely perish since we have no knowledge of the sea or navigation.

I can assure you this will not happen. You will and must remain with our men until the last one is dead and we will be the last to die. I inform you that you are arrested and confined to your cabin." I turned him over to Lt. Briede and Corporal von Lutzow who had been sick but had the strength to ensure that the captain was securely confined. Then I went back on deck to further encourage the men. The corporals came back and told me the captain had tried all kinds of tricks and pleas to get out of the cabin by conspiring with the helmsman. The corporals came again and reported the captain wanted to relieve himself and get out of the cabin. I refused and told him he could do it in the cabin which was already soaked anyhow. I went to the cabin and implored him to be silent and go to sleep. He and the helmsman had some kind of secret conversation. I demanded he be silent in the cabin.

I reported all this to the Lt. Col. who was very ill. He approved of what I had done and requested I try a do whatever was necessary to sustain our men since he felt very ill and could not come on deck.

16 Sept: Finally day broke and we saw the really miserable condition of the ship, what a loss we had suffered and that we were in grave danger. All our food supplies, fresh vegetables, four lambs for the sick, and cattle, etc. were lost overboard or lay dead in a corner of the ship. A large anchor was lost. The ship's boats that had come loose were all smashed and useless. We threw them in the sea. Since there was no chance for escape, we let the captain free. We remained in this sad condition until midday when the wind abated somewhat and the sea and waves calmed and became smaller. No one can really describe such a miserable experience with enough emphasis and only those who actually experienced it can really comprehend.

17 Sept: The sky gradually cleared and the wind remained from the north. We observed at midday that we're located at 37 degrees 19' latitude [East of Cape Charles, Virginia]. We had been gradually pushed far south in the storm. But how far east in the ocean were we? The ship's captain was not skilled enough to determine our longitude and it can't be determined accurately anyhow. Our first priority was to clean up the ropes, sails and spars and to clear the gunwales and go into the hold to inspect the damage and look for leaks. We rejoiced in not finding any! The men came on deck to dry out their things but no one had a dry stitch of clothing. Everything was soaked and covered with a black slime and dirt. Most of the barrels and chests of food were spoiled much to the dismay of the ship's cook. The cartridges were all sort of stuck together and unusable. In short everything

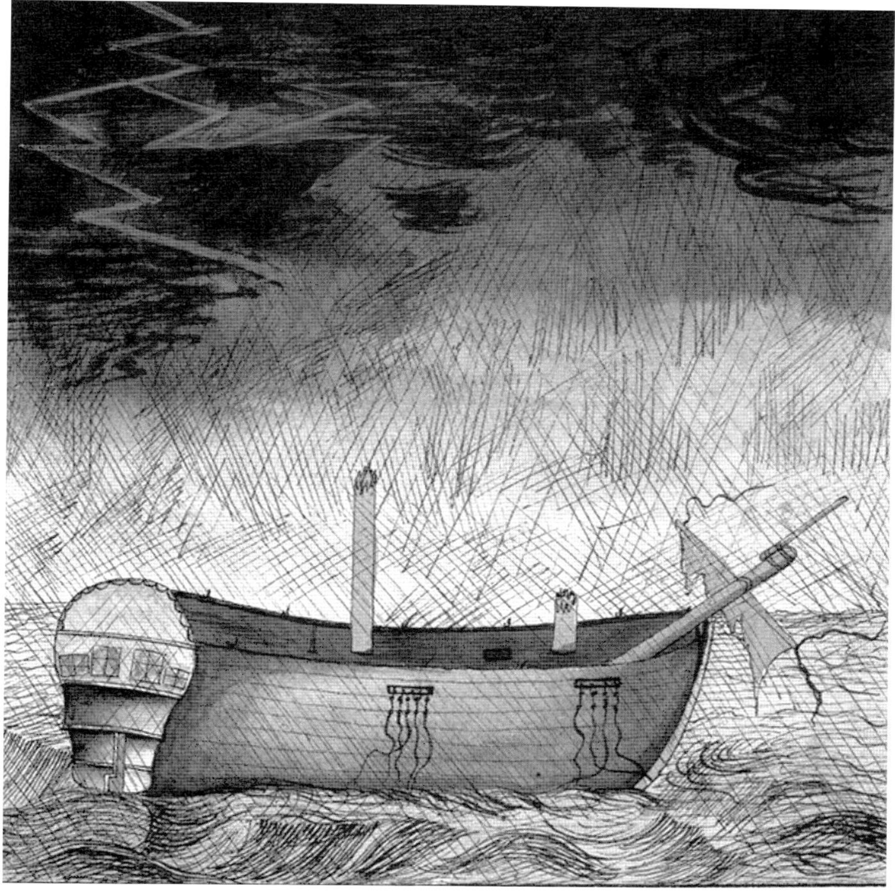

Triton after the storm. *University of Pennsylvania Library.*

was ruined. The crew sought out some old discarded sails and fashioned them together on an old topmast with nails and rope. This served as a jury rigged mast for the stump of the old main mast as good as possible so that we could make some headway when the wind became favorable again.

18 Sept: Weather was fair and clear and wind from the northeast. We sailed to 37 degrees 25' latitude just a bit from our position yesterday [East of Hog Island Bay, Virginia]. Our crew tried to overhaul the rigged mast and get a temporary fix for the foremast and furled sails there.

19 Sept: Beautiful clear morning followed by some clouds. Wind was from the northwest and our course southwest until 8:00 when we steered north by east. With good weather the men had cleaned up a bit and did the most needed work on the ship. We held a proper service in which we thanked the Almighty God for our salvation and sang hymn 449 and read the 107 Psalm out loud. This all occurred with heartfelt piety and sincere thanks. Even the ships boys who understood none of this held their silence and piously listened and prayed to themselves. At about 6:00 p.m. we discovered a ship from the north about three leagues away. She appeared to have lost her top mast as well. I loaded the swivel gun which still remained intact and let loose two shots. We unfurled the British jack as an emergency sign and made as much sail towards her as possible to see whether friend or foe. Night fell before we could reach her. We put out a lantern to let her know we wished to be seen and to join up with her. Due to the darkness we were not able to determine whether he was friend of foe. The helmsman asked what we should do if he was the enemy and we were attacked. I answered that we would fight force with force. If we had to flee we would deceive the enemy in the following way. If we were chased by a privateer or a French ship we would get all the soldiers below. If we were hailed and questioned about our origin, destination or cargo we would say we were from England bound for New York and had cargo aboard and were damaged in the recent storm. A privateer would board us with ten or twelve men and attempt to capture our ship. We would grab them as soon as they came on board and hold them prisoner. This would prevent the privateer vessel from firing his cannons at us to avoid killing his own men. We must hold our place. They will not try to board us anyhow since we have an overwhelming majority of troops with which we could hold them off. The helmsman agreed and I proposed the same to Col. Heymell who did not disagree. I went on deck and ordered the junior officers that when the privateer closed us I would give a sign with a stab of my fist. They should jump out and catch the privateer's men and not engage them further. They should avoid a conflict with them. All the remaining soldiers should remain hidden below decks until I gave further orders. However, the ship had disappeared from view and despite all the preparations we did not a get a chance to put our plan in effect.

20 Sept: It was a pleasant morning although the night had been very dark with strong lightning. The wind was north by northeast. At about 9:00 AM we spied a ship directly ahead running up on us. We were pleased since we believed her to be an English frigate or some other friendly ship on an ocean crossing that could tow us back to Sandy Hook. Thus we showed our ship's colors but the other ship sailed right on by. Thus we could not determine if she were friend or foe. She continued straight on her course without paying us any attention. Around noon the wind changed to north by east and our course went west by north. The seas were very deep and the ship rocked back and forth and from side to side.

21 Sept: Last night was very rough and the morning was overcast and cloudy. The seas were deep and rough. We were at about 38 degrees latitude [east of Assateague Island] *but we could not get an accurate reckoning without sun shining. Our course was WNW with NNE wind.*

23 Sept: Somewhat clearer with lighter wind NE by E and our course NW by N. We reckoned to be at 38 degrees 14 minutes latitude [just southeast of Ocean City, Maryland]. *At about 10:00 a.m. we discovered a schooner dead ahead. She stood in for the coast and was soon out of sight. By noon we were at 38 degrees 26' latitude having travelled 12'* [southern tip of Delaware near Rehoboth] *in 24 hours. An hour later we saw another ship dead ahead and believed it to be the same schooner we had seen earlier.*

24 Sept: This morning it rained but soon cleared up. The sea water was no longer green by gray-white in color. We supposed ourselves thus to be near the shore. At 8:00 a.m. we took soundings and were at 20 fathoms depth. At noon we had 16.5 fathoms and at 2:00 p.m. 17 fathoms. By 3:00 p.m. we changed course to north by east.

25 Sept: At daybreak we were at the mouth of the Delaware River, so close, that we could make out the Capes. The weather was especially fair and the wind blew WSW and we sailed NE away from the shore to avoid privateers and make for the open sea. We did not [know] *exactly where we were but with such a favorable wind we headed for Sandy Hook which was 24 hours away even with our tattered sails. We wished each other the best of luck since we had avoided the privateers up to this point. The crew was promised some extra pay if they would strive to be vigilant through the night and get us to Sandy Hook the next day. I stayed on deck nearly all night to encourage the crew and in order to keep them going gave them two bottles of wine to drink. The wind was especially fair until midnight when we became becalmed.*

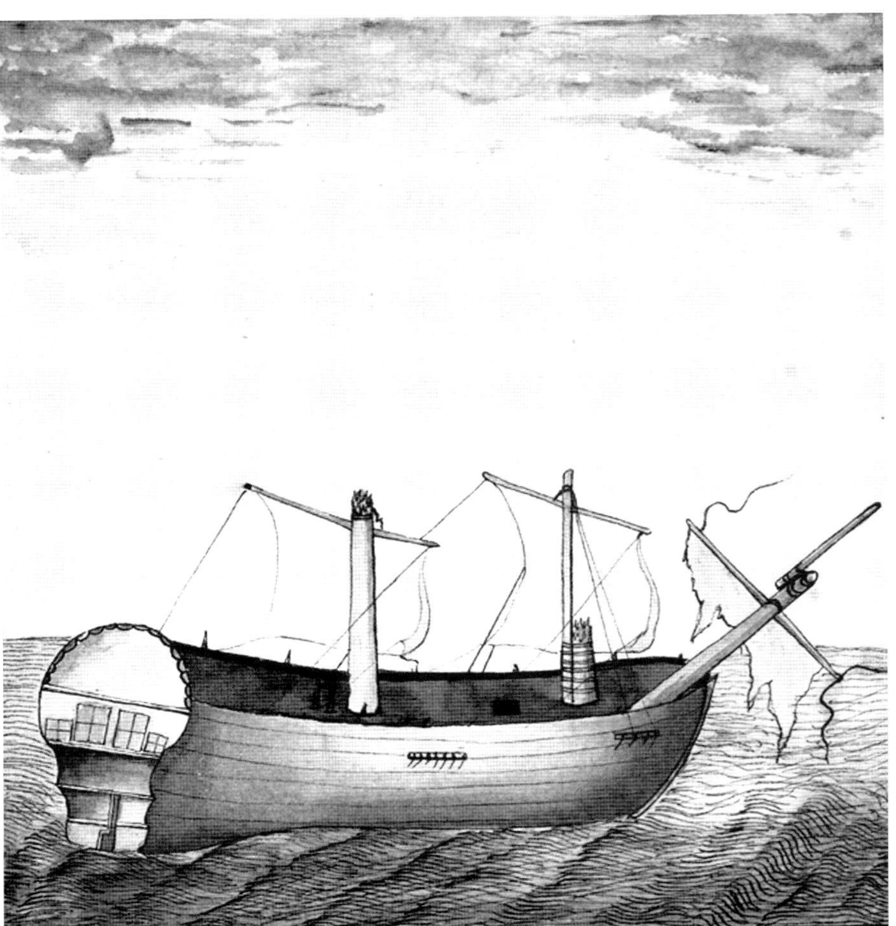

Triton captured. *University of Pennsylvania Library.*

Then the fateful day arrived:

26 Sept: A very beautiful morning but a sad and unlucky day. At daybreak, I saw relatively far off, two sails to the windward. I jumped for joy up into the captain's cabin to inform Col. Heymell and the other officers. We went on deck and complimented ourselves that they were out of NY and sent to the aid of ships damaged in the hurricane. As mentioned the two ships came at us from the green sea (windward) and not from the enemy's shore to the leeward. They could bring us into the harbor and protect us from swarming Capers (privateers). We were in miserable condition and according to the captain were in no way able to maneuver or escape. We kept the two ships in close view since they were pursuing us. Nevertheless, we still believed they were coming to aid us in distress and offer assistance. But oh! We were totally betrayed in our hope as they came near enough for us to see the thirteen striped red and white ensigns flying. Our joy morphed into sadness. I had to relay orders from Col. Heymell to the captain and helmsman (since the captain was sick). Could we come about or escape? Both assured us that this was impossible. We had to rely on ourselves and could not put our previous plans for deception into play since there were two privateers who could overwhelm us or sink us easily. It was scarcely 8:00 AM and they were alongside us. On the starboard was Schooner Mars *with fourteen cannons commanded by Captain Taylor and to the port the Shallop* Comet *with ten cannons commanded by Captain Decatur. Both ships were heavily manned. The hailed our helmsman to lower the sail and put the helm hard to starboard which he did. They then lowered a boat and boarded us with a lieutenant and five crewmen. We were lashed to the Schooner* Mars *and towed to Barnegat Inlet where we anchored. The shallop lay near us but the schooner on which the* Triton's *captain and three of our sailors had been taken sailed continuously onward. (Col. Heymell had wished to join them but due to his illness was too weak)*

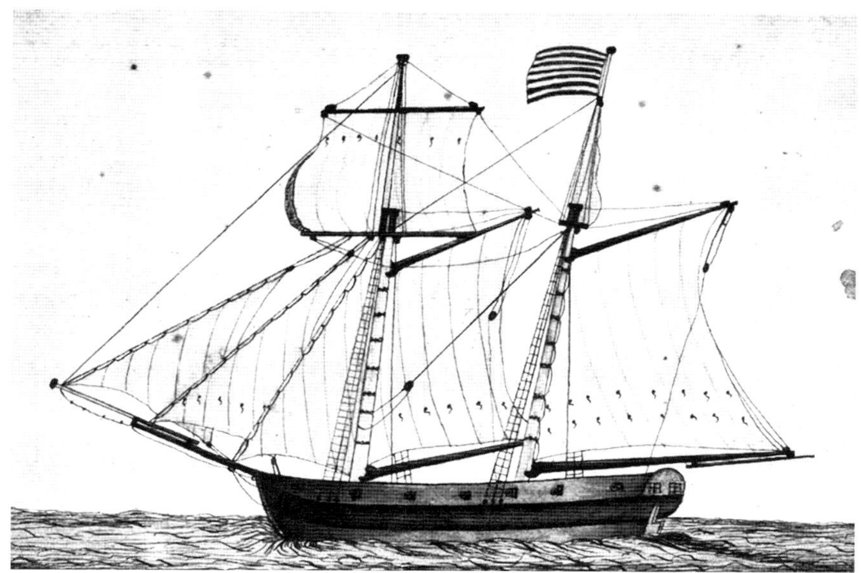

Schooner *Mars. University of Pennsylvania Library.*

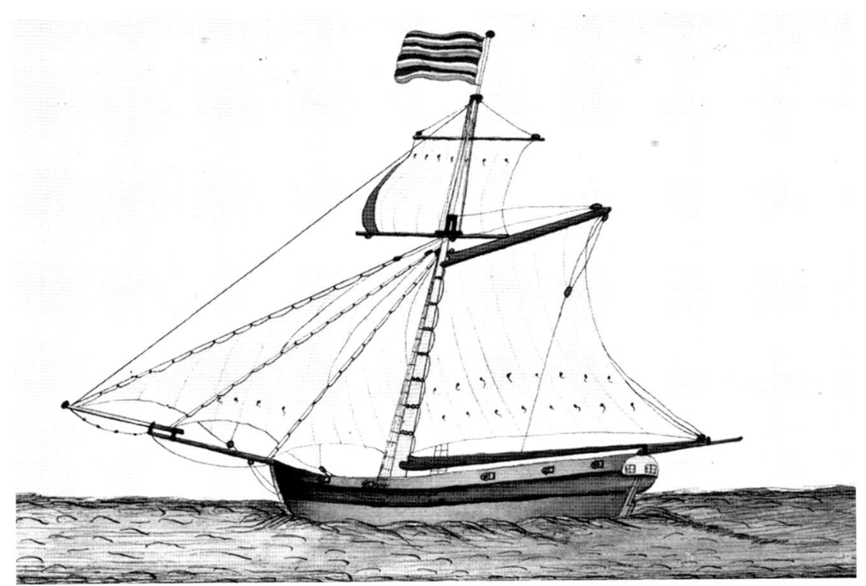

Sloop *Comet. University of Pennsylvania Library.*

I am not sure why but no farther than two gunshots away the schooner Mars *ran aground on a shoal. The wind and waves were strong and despite all efforts to float her she capsized right before our eyes. Everything fell overboard and the crew stood on the keel of the overturned ship parallel to the surface of the water. The waves relentlessly struck the ship until three more privateers nearby lowered their boats and saved the crew. The crew had to swim to the boats but the waves prevented the boats from getting too close to the capsized schooner. Two men drowned. Had the privateers been less honorable and polite and not left Co. Heymell on our ship he would have died miserably. If this whole thing had occurred at night the crew would have drowned and we would have gained our freedom.*

27 Sept: Weather was beautiful but a thick fog surrounded our moods and hearts when we thought about our current and future misery. At 10:00 a.m. the anchor was weighed and the intention of the privateers was to tow us to the Delaware Bay and up to Philadelphia, but a distant ship to the SW changed their minds since they thought her to be an English vessel. So we were pulled along to the mouth of Little Egg Harbor until nightfall. They anchored due to the frequent sandbars. Our ship ran aground but freed herself each time.

28 Sept: Another beautiful morning and at 6:30 a.m. the anchor was weighed but soon redeployed since they were not sure of the area.

29 Sept: We ran into Little Egg Harbor and anchored again.

The captain of the *Mars* was the renowned American privateer Yelverton Taylor, one of the most prolific privateer captains from the Delaware Bay region. The captain of the *Comet* was Stephen Decatur Sr. (1751–1808), the father of the more famous naval officer Commodore Stephen Decatur of Barbary pirate fame. Born in Rhode Island, Decatur lived most of his life in Philadelphia and commanded five privateers during the Revolution. Decatur was eventually offered a captaincy in the U.S. Navy in 1798. He then saw action as commander of the ship *Delaware* in the Quasi-War against France. He is buried with his son Stephen Jr. in St. Peter's Church, Philadelphia.

Andreas Wiederholdt and his band of Hessians were marched from Little Egg Harbor Bay to Pennsylvania across South Jersey, and he found some parts of the journey interesting.

On October 3, Wiederholdt disembarked and arrived at Egg Harbor Forks, which was an important stopping-off village for privateers on the way to western New Jersey to sell their captured prizes. The "Forks," as they are called, were at the confluence of the Mullica and Batsto Rivers near a town called Sweetwater.

Here he makes a rather sarcastic observation:

Reiffurth and Lieutenant Briede joined us with our troops who had gone to Chestnut Neck. The troops had to lie down in stables and sheds as no other place was available for them. Still they were happy to leave the miserable ship and to be on God's earth if American earth is God's earth.

What follows here is a vivid and remarkable description by Wiederholdt of South Jersey barrier islands, marsh and bay lands and a bit of the lives of people who inhabited them in the eighteenth century.

October 4: …Here I must make (since it is a rest day) some observations about the famous and fatal Egg Harbor. In reality it isn't a harbor at all but an expansive place with sandbars, shoals, swamps, morasses and small sandy islands. Through these wind channels or passages, so that a ship of little draught can manage by ebb tide. The channels are so narrow that in many places a ship can only pass by staying in the middle. In others one can sail so close to the shore that one can reach out and touch the banks with one's hand. If a boatman is unfamiliar with these channels or does not have a good pilot it is impossible to pass through. This is so even though one can see another boat at 1,000 paces away. There are so many curves and turns, one after the other that a boat would run aground even where one imagines a large ship is capable of navigating. I experienced all this myself when trying to navigate towards a house and ran aground until a ships boy steered us off with his oar and directed us to the right channel.

The people who live on the scattered islands are pilots who guide ships through the channels and earn a living fishing. The islands are of poor soil, sandy and swampy so that not much grows except scrub cedar, pine and marsh grass and reeds. Some of the ground around their houses is cultivated with soil amended with dung fertilizer which only supports miserable vegetables. They have a few livestock which graze on the marsh grass. The inhabitants must obtain wood, grain and other necessities from the mainland. The homes are all surrounded by dams and ditches which constantly need replenishing or clearing out to protect the houses from floods or gales from the nearby ocean. In the entrance to this so-called harbor it is teaming with shoals so that in ordinary weather it appears frightful when waves break upon them. It is very dangerous to sail in there when the wind is blowing off the sea towards land and the spray shoots up creating giant figures above the land. We experienced this danger ourselves with the American ship [Mars] grounded and avoided grounding ourselves four more times. The entrance between the shoals and the first islands into the harbor is in some spots barely 20 paces wide. So I believe that in this dangerous place the English navy could easily create a blockade by sinking a few vessels.

A creek is a water way that connects channels with each other or the sea. It is subject to ebb and flood tides but cannot really be called a river or stream. Another type of waterway is called a run which is not affected so much by tides. Runs can be impossible to cross when it rains or snows come from the hills but can be waded through or passed by small boats.

A schooner is a small ship with two masts that draws very little water, sails very fast and can easily be steered. It can get through almost any channel since they only require 4–5 feet of water to float.

A sloop is about the same construction but with only one mast and usually smaller than the schooner. Both are the type of ships for privateers along the mainland shore and amongst the islands.

Between October 6 and 15, the Hessian party arrived in Philadelphia after having traveled through Haddonfield, through which they had marched when evacuating Philadelphia the previous year. They were quartered at the Golden Swan Inn at Third and Arch Streets. Soon they were taken before the Board of War and commanded to remove to Reading, Pennsylvania, where they arrived on the fifteenth. Wiederholdt took private lodgings for a guinea per month in Reading, which at the time consisted of about three hundred houses.

It was not until July 1780 that the Hessians were exchanged, and they left Reading, crossing the Delaware at London's Ferry. From Elizabethtown, they boarded two sloops and were ferried to New York.

Very little is known about the ultimate fate of Andreas Wiederholdt. According to Burgoyne, he was born in Spangenberg, Hesse, in 1732–33. After the Revolutionary War, he became a general officer in the Portuguese army.

The Wiederholdt diary once possessed by Mr. J.G. Rosengarten states that Andreas Wiederholdt died in Kassel as a major in 1805. The Rosengarten copy was donated to the University of Pennsylvania in 1924 and is housed in their Rare Book Collection. The original of the diary was given to Wiederholdt's son and eventually grandson, who immigrated to America in 1880. The sketches Andreas Wiederholdt made while on his sea voyage of the *Triton, Mars* and *Comet* are included here by permission of the Library of the University of Pennsylvania.

6

TROUBLE ON THE HOMEFRONT

J.P. HAND

It is very difficult for a modern-day American citizen to imagine the emotional turmoil felt by an eighteenth-century British subject living in America when required to decide whether to remain loyal to the king or join neighbors, friends and family who were prepared to commit treason. Aside from the inborn loyalty to "God, King, and Country" and the sheer newness of the idea of independence and self-determination, the social and legal ramifications of the decision must have been overwhelming. Whether English or foreign-born, or first-, second- or third-generation American, the concept of allegiance to a sovereign and the representatives of the same was as constant as the rising and setting of the sun (the English Civil Wars excepted).

In the case of the inhabitants of Cape May, as in the rest of New Jersey and throughout the colonies, making the wrong choice could have serious consequences. For those who chose to join the fight for independence, the failure of that effort meant the possibility of the loss of life, liberty and—possibly of more importance to one's offspring—the loss of property. As it happened, that was the reality of those who chose to remain loyal to their king and country. As unfair as it may seem to us today, many otherwise law-abiding Americans lost their lands due to the fact that the patriarch of their family made the wrong choice.

One important detail regarding Cape May in the struggle for independence is the fact that the county's inhabitants, almost to the person, were loyal to the Patriot cause. No other New Jersey county could make that claim. The neighboring counties of Cumberland, Salem and Gloucester had a surprisingly large number of Tories. The counties to the north had populations that were divided along political lines as well. That isn't to say that the burden was shared equally among the adult male population of Cape May County. A few years into the war, on May 27, 1778, eighty-seven county men signed the Oath of Allegiance to the new state government, which seems to indicate that a significant portion of the county's prominent citizens were still in favor of breaking ties with their mother country. More revealing though are the rosters that name the Cape May men who served in the state and/or Continental troops and the county militia. In addition, contemporary newspaper accounts, surviving ledgers and receipt books containing the names of Cape May's privateer officers, crewmen and investors round out the list of county residents with "skin in the game."

These records reveal that most of the officers of the Cape May Militia during the Revolution were from a handful of families, in particular the Hand family and their Stillwell cousins. Members of these families, along with others connected to them through marriage—the Willetses, Stiteses, Corsons, Holmeses and Somerses—also made up the lion's share of the privateer captains, officers and investors from the region. Men of fighting age from some very large and very prominent families of Cape May County are noticeably absent in the records mentioned. The Hildreths, Eldredges and Crowells and others may have been in favor of independence or were at least quietly neutral, but they don't appear to have taken a very active part in the conflict. Other Cape May families, such as the Hugheses, Matthewses and Schellingers, were underrepresented in comparison to the families' numbers and stature in the county. Those same families mentioned were for the most part from early whaling families from the lower end of the county who were Baptists or Presbyterians and had for generations had no qualms about standing muster or serving in the local militia when called upon.

Ironically, many of the Cape May men who were members of the Society of Friends served in the county militia and as privateers over the course of the war. Since the beginning of the church in the mid-seventeenth century, the Friends have held nonviolence as a central tenet of their faith. These Quakers, as their Calvinist and secular neighbors referred to them, had the British authorities and Loyalists to fear and also risked being "read out of meeting, excommunicated or expelled" for service that in any way related to bearing arms against their fellow man.

From its inception in 1692 and through the Revolution, Cape May County was divided into three precincts or townships: the Upper, Middle and Lower Townships. Beginning with the arrival of the earliest whaler-yeomen on the Cape, almost all of the Quakers settled in the Upper Township. The Friends were never a dominant force in the county, and the turmoil caused by the patriotic fervor of young Quaker men coupled with the romantic inclinations of both sexes to marry outside of the church led to a quick decline of the Society of Friends in the county. The argument can be made that the upheaval in society caused by seven years of armed conflict against Britain was one of the two main causes of that decline. The second, the death knell so to speak, was the rapid spread of the Methodist Episcopal Church throughout Cape May County and the rest of West Jersey.

The following entries from the Great Egg Harbour Monthly Meeting Minutes reveal the cultural and religious challenges that young men from local Quaker families faced with the onset of hostilities with Great Britain:

10-6-1777   *Richard Townsend has now gone out with the militia into the war.*

6-14-1779   *Darius Corson of Cape May has joined others in taking and making a prize of an English vessel and cargo lately caste away here.*

12-3-1781   *Thomas Townsend has joined a company in privateering and gone to sea.*

1-6-1783   *Clement Cordrey has taken up arms against the people called refugees* [the term used for Tory privateers].

Those meeting minutes also indicate that many of the Revolutionary-era Quakers from both sides of the Egg Harbor Bay were removed from the church for marrying out of unity (marriage to non-Quakers) or for marrying their first or second cousins (a practice that was quite common among the mostly Baptist or Presbyterian population of Cape May County).

Interestingly, the most prominent and possibly the wealthiest Quaker in the region, Colonel Richard Somers, doesn't appear to have been read out of meeting, even though he not only served as a militia colonel but also was a major supplier of munitions and arms to the local militias. In addition, he served as the banker for much of the Cape May–Philadelphia privateer trade. To add insult to injury, Somers married Sophia Stillwell, the daughter of Nicholas Stillwell Sr. and Sarah Hand, both of whom were from non-Quaker families from the lower end of the Cape. It seems that Richard

Somers's wealth and prominence in his community may have insulated him from the standards to which the rest of his congregation was subject.

Keep in mind that by the time of the Revolution, the relatively small population of Cape May shared a homogeneous culture based on the traditions and values of the English yeoman. Most of the county's inhabitants were the descendants of immigrants from the British Isles. Those county natives with non-English surnames, the Corsons, Schellingers, Steelmans and so on, were the descendants of early Dutch and Swedish immigrants who had long ago married into Anglo families and for all intents and purposes had become English. At the time of European settlement there were very few Native Americans living on the Jersey Cape and the county's small African American population, whether slave or free, were sharing the same traditions regarding religion, diet and dress as the county's residents of European descent.

We can speculate as to what the American Patriots hoped to gain if their efforts to achieve independence were successful. Obviously, for rich and poor alike, many aspects of their lives were controlled by the powers that be in the mother country far across the Atlantic. For the American colonists, including those in Cape May, that's the way it had always been. As for the risks involved, we don't have to speculate; the many surviving newspaper accounts, letters and journals make clear the attitude that the British had toward the American traitors.

The perfect example of this may have been the threat posed by British lieutenant colonel Charles Mawhood in a letter to Cape May native Colonel Elijah Hand of the Cumberland County militia (see appendix Item 3). In that letter, the British officer threatened to burn the houses of many of the most prominent men of the town of Salem, New Jesery, if Colonel Hand and his men didn't surrender their arms and return home. Mawhood then listed those seventeen men of Salem, including Thomas Sinnickson, a wealthy militia officer and major investor in the privateer schooner *Hawk* (see chapter 4), and fellow officer Captain Nicholas Kean, who also shared command of various state gunboats and privateer vessels with Colonel Elijah Hand.

THE TROUBLE ON THE HOMEFRONT

The war years from 1775 to 1783 affected most every aspect of life for Cape May County's soldiers, privateers and civilians alike. The local population had to deal with inflated currency, shortages of essential imports and the threat of harm befalling loved ones serving the new republic on land or at sea. In addition to those issues, the inhabitants of Cape May experienced the general upheaval of societal norms that are seen in any community during wartime. Whether friend or foe, transients in the county compounded that upheaval, as did the county's particularly vulnerable location as a peninsula surrounded by water on three sides and located by sea between Philadelphia and New York.

A careful study of the court records and newspaper accounts of the time reveals that the disorder brought about by seven years of armed conflict was more complicated than one might think. For the soldiers and privateers in particular, there were other issues to contend with in addition to the possibility of armed conflict with British troops, naval vessels and Loyalists.

For instance, the court records of Cape May County leading up to the Revolution (1692–1775) contain the typical lawsuits—debt being by far the most common issue—as well as the occasional charge of trespass, assault and battery, slander and so forth. The same can be said of neighboring Cumberland and Gloucester Counties. Those court records clearly show that cases involving assault and battery and, to a lesser degree, adultery, rose dramatically in the years shortly before, during and just after the war.

Surprisingly, even those we might call the elite of the county—prominent merchants, militia officers and privateer captains—appear to have been more than willing to settle their differences with their fists. As to what caused the spike in assault cases in Cape May during the rebellion isn't clear, whether the disputes were centered on political differences or were just the common neighborly disagreements that have always plagued mankind. Perhaps the ready availability of captured British rum and other spirits played a part in it. The fact is that the list of Cape May men charged with assault during this time reads as a virtual who's-who of the county's privateer captains and crew.

Of the twenty-three documented privateer captains of Cape May County, at least five were charged with assault between the years 1779 and 1781. Among those were Joseph Edwards Jr., Moses Griffing, Enoch Stillwell, Enoch Willets and James Willets Jr. The charge of assault lodged against Captain Enoch Stillwell in 1780 may have been a case of alleged workplace violence. During Stillwell's jury trial, "John Erixson" gave evidence for the defense, while of the three witnesses for the state, Abraham Bennet and Richard Stites were fellow privateers and Nathaniel Foster was a militia officer (also charged with assault during the war). Enoch Stillwell's testimony and that of his witnesses must have been convincing, as the jury found him not guilty.

Some of the other notable incidents are recounted here:

A few years before the war began, Irish Protestant immigrant John Holmes arrived in Cape May with his three younger brothers, Thomas, Nathaniel and James. Within a decade, he had become a very prosperous merchant and landowner. Holmes was one of the wealthiest men in Cape May County at the time of his death in 1791. He was also a major privateer investor and held a large stake in the schooner *Hawk*. In 1787, John Holmes was charged with assault, opted for a jury trial and was found not guilty by a jury of his peers (including ex-privateers Matthew Hand and Nicholas Stillwell).

Before leaving his brothers at Cape May to settle in Galloway Township, Gloucester County (where he married a tavern owner's daughter and opened his own tavern), James Holmes was charged with assault and battery against Edward Church by the court at Cape May. Holmes was also indicted for fornication with Rhoda Jenkins before departing the county. After receiving an officer's commission (Gloucester militia and Continental army), Captain James Holmes was severely wounded at the Battle of Princeton and was allegedly carried off of the battlefield on General Washington's horse. He returned to his wife and tavern and died of the effects of his wounds a few years later.

The apparently "rowdy" privateer Joseph Edwards Jr. was indicted for assault and battery in 1779 and fornication at the February 1780 term.

John Grace (private and Continental troops), the man General Washington referred to as "my trusted scout whom British gold cannot buy," was called before a grand jury to answer for the charge of assault, along with fellow county residents Henry Young, David Gandy and John Britton.

The celebrated Delaware Bay pilot Matthew Hand, who was credited with saving Captain Stephen Decatur Sr. and his vessel on the open sea, was charged with assault no fewer than three times. In his defense, two of the incidents occurred almost ten years apart, in 1775 and 1784, and involved the same injured party, Jonathan Cresse, so there was obviously some bad blood between the two. Matthew pled guilty to the first charge and was found guilty by a jury of the second assault. In the first case, "The King vs Matthew Hand," he was fined a paltry six pence. In the second case, "The State vs Matthew Hand," the fine levied was six dollars and court fees. Five years after the war ended, Matthew was charged with the same offense for a third time against Carman Richardson and merchant and privateer moneyman George Taylor. Those who gave evidence for the state included the two alleged victims and Uriah Smith.

This time, Matthew Hand came armed with his own witnesses, including ex-privateer Nathaniel Holmes, Ferdinand Newton and Lydia McCoy at one hearing and Jeremiah Hand and Seth Hand at another. After hearing all of the evidence, the jury found Matthew not guilty. If any character in this story could be described as "swashbuckling," it is surely Matthew Hand, who also served as an officer on board the privateer schooner *Hawk* (ten guns, fifty men). In 1779, Matthew sued his distant cousin Lieutenant Colonel Enoch Stillwell for nonpayment of his share of prize vessels, the British brig *Lyon* and the schooner *Henry*, for the princely sum of £3,000. The case was settled in the New Jersey Supreme Court, where it appears that Matthew Hand received his due.

In the years prior to hostilities with Great Britain, cases of assault and battery recorded by the county courts were relatively few and far between. That all changed during the course of the war. The names of additional Cape May men who were charged with assault during this time include the following:

> *Assault and Battery, Cape May County Quarterly Court*
> *1776, John B. McCormack*
> *1779, Moses Griffing, Enoch Willits, Joseph Edwards Jr.*
> *1780, Joseph Wheaton, Daniel Hand, Jr., Rueben Foster, Nathaniel Foster, John Eldredge Jr., Hosea Eldredge, Daniel Stites, John McMahon, Enoch Stillwell, Jeremiah Edmunds, William Hawkings, Thomas Burgess, (against both George Hollinshead and John Ructan), William Mitchell*
> *Undated, Isaac Day, Ellis Hand, William Martin, Richard Steelman, and Zephaniah Steelman*

Cumberland County's General Silas Newcomb, commanding officer of all of the county militias in West Jersey during the Revolution, was charged with assault. That incident occurred back in the year 1771 when he was known as "Captain Newcomb"—he had previously served as Cumberland's county sheriff.

Romance at Old Cape May

While it is very clear that personal violence between the inhabitants of Cape May rose considerably around the time of the Revolution, it could also be said that the number of romances, both legitimate and illicit, rose in the county as well.

The most celebrated romantic tale of colonial Cape May is the story of militia colonel and privateer captain Nicholas Stillwell Jr. and his sweetheart, Ruhamah Hand. As the story goes, a few years before the war broke out (1771), Ruhamah grew tired of waiting for Nicholas to marry her and agreed to marry another local young man, Henry Ludlam. Upon hearing the news, the young militia captain raced to the scene of the wedding, which was allegedly in Philadelphia (not that uncommon for young Cape May couples of the merchant class). On the morning of the wedding, Nicholas asked Ruhamah to marry him instead. She spurned her betrothed and agreed to marry her old suitor. According to family lore, Ruhamah believed that many of the heartbreaks in her life, the deaths of some of her children at a young age and the loss of her husband at the age of fifty, were the result of her actions of that day.

Some of the lesser-known love stories of Revolutionary War–era Cape May would be lost to history if not for the carefully preserved court records located in the Cape May County Clerk's Office. Sometimes the briefest notation in a court ledger can tell a lot, such as the aforementioned case where recent Irish Protestant immigrant James Holmes was indicted for fornication with Rhoda Jenkins, who was descended from one of the earliest families on the Cape.

Rhoda Jenkins wasn't the only young woman of colonial Cape May to be charged with the "crime" of engaging in premarital sex. In the years just prior to the Revolution, Lydia Foster, Hannah Hewitt, Elizabeth Richardson and Jane Hand were charged with fornication as well. All were descendants of original settlers at Cape May, and the outcome of their cases is

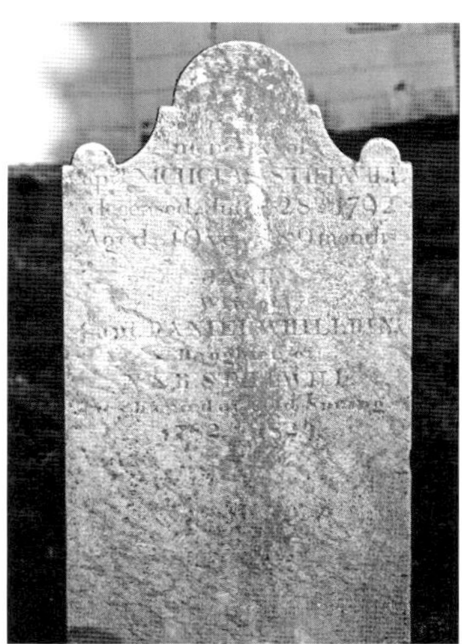

Captain Nicholas Stillwell, Cornelius Hand burial ground (Fairview Cemetery), Cape May Court House, New Jersey. *Photo by Jim Talone.*

unclear, with the exception of Jane Hand, who was accused of "fornication with some man to the jury unknown." While we can only imagine how the jury came to their decision, Jane Hand was found not guilty.

Those court records occasionally refute family history and local lore, as in the case of the celebrated privateer Captain Humphrey Hughes and Jane Whilldin. The author of *The Mayflower Descendants of Cape May County* as well as many family genealogies record the couple as being married in the year 1774 (without giving a day or month or listing a source).

At odds with this information is an entry in the original Cape May County Court ledger for the years 1774–90. Under the heading "Pleas of the Crown February Term 1776" is listed an indictment charging Humphrey Hughes and "Jean Whilden" with fornication. That term was used to describe the crime of consensual sex between unmarried adults and usually indicates the pregnancy of a single woman. *The Mayflower Descendants* also lists one child, Humphrey Hughes Jr., born to the couple on November 20, 1775, just a few years before the young privateer captain was lost at sea aboard the privateer sloop *New Comet* along with his twenty-five-man crew. That record suggests that Humphrey and Jane weren't married in 1774, and if a wedding did take place, it may have been prompted by the charges filed in 1776. In fact, it appears that the couple never married. When Jane Whilldin's father, James Whilldin Esq., died in 1780, he left a will that contains some telling lines:

> *Item I also further will and Direct that Whereas my Son James Whilden, in Consideration of my bequeathing to him and his heirs a larger Proportion of my Estate than to others of my children; do pay or cause to be paid to my Grandson Seth Whilden the sum of Forty pounds Currency of New Jersey…as soon as he shall attain the age of Twenty One Years and in the meantime take care of, bring up, Educate, Support & maintain him the said Seth till he attains the age of fourteen years & then to Procure him some good Trade*
>
> *Item And my Will further is for the same Consideration that he likewise bring up, take care of, educate, Support & Maintain the son of my Daughter Jane commonly known by the name of Humphrey Hughes, until he shall attain the Age of Fourteen years & then procure him some good Trade & at the time He shall attain to the Age of Twenty One Years that he pay to the said Humphrey Hughes the Sum of Twenty pounds.*

James Whilldin Sr. Esq. was a prominent landowner, merchant and magistrate who left movable property valued at over £35,000, a figure that didn't include his substantial real estate holdings. He and two of his fellow justices at Cape May were the longtime antagonists of the despised (Royal Customs) "Collector of Salem and Cohansy" John Hatton. Whilldin was also a member of the Cape May Committee of Safety at the outbreak of the Revolution. The wording used in his will suggests that his five-year-old grandson, Humphrey, was born out of wedlock. While no date is known for the death of Captain Hughes and his crew, it is believed to have occurred sometime between November 9, 1778, when letters of marque were issued for the privateer sloop *New Comet*, "Master, Humphrey Hughes," and July 17, 1780, the date that the mother of his child, Jane Whilldin, married Jeremiah Edmunds of Cape May (New Jersey State archives, Colonial Marriage Bonds). The marriage bond lists the bride by her maiden name. In addition to her son, "commonly known by the name of Humphrey Hughes," Jane would bear four children by her husband, Jeremiah.

In another instance, where the information seems to jump from the page, the story is much more complex than it would seem. In 1794, a little more than a decade after the war ended, this entry was written into the court ledger:

The Grand Jury Came into Court and Presented the following Bills
The State vs
Matthew Hand for Adultery
Rachel Taylor for Fornication
George Hand for Adultery
Sarah Stites for Adultery
Experience Smith for Adultery
Abigail Edwards for Adultery
Enos Buck for Adultery
Richard Shaw for Adultery
Ebenezer Ingersoll for Perjury?

From this entry it would appear that there was a "new sheriff in town" who wanted to clean up the community, but things weren't as bad as they appear. In colonial America, it was extremely rare for a divorce to be granted. Some of these individuals had been long separated from their legal spouses and had no choice but to commit the crime of "adultery" if they chose to enter into a new relationship.

The case of Matthew Hand and Sarah Hand Stites is a good example of that predicament. In 1794, the Delaware Bay pilot and ex-privateer officer was a forty-year-old widower with six children. Sarah had left her husband, Benjamin Stites III (they had one daughter who died before reaching adulthood), and obtaining a divorce was not an option, despite the fact that her late father, Daniel Hand, had been among the most influential inhabitants of the county. Interestingly, though Matthew and Sarah shared the same last name, she was actually more closely related to her estranged husband, Benjamin, than she was to Matthew Hand.

Matthew Hand and Sarah Hand Stites would live together as man and wife with his children by his first wife. In addition, they would have two sons together, Hand Stites and Page Stites (who was known as Page Hand until he reached legal age). Apparently, the custom or law of the time required illegitimate children to carry the name of their mother's legal spouse. Sarah was deceased by the year 1812, when Matthew Hand (now fifty-eight years of age) married Rhoda Allen Hughes, the recent widow (six months) of wealthy Cape Island tavern keeper and landowner Memucan Hughes. Rhoda was Hughes's second wife and was not the mother of his children. Hughes was apparently not very fond of his second wife, whom he left "all household goods she brought at our marriage, said goods to be made as good as when she brought it…also a black boy named, Maskel, until he is 25 (on April 20, 1826), when he is to be freed."

So, late in life Matthew Hand inadvertently became a slave owner, assuming that his new wife didn't free Maskel immediately. Matthew and Rhoda had no children together, but in 1815, after being married for about two or three years, they adopted by indenture Adeline Rankins (age four years, seven months), the daughter of single mother Sally Rankins. Little Adeline may have been the illegitimate daughter of Matthew Hand. In his 1828 will, Matthew referred to Adeline as his daughter and left her an equal share of his estate. Interestingly, Matthew left all of his surviving children one-seventh of his estate, but only Adeline and his other surviving "natural" child, Page Stites, inherited personal items named in the will.

One case from the Cape May court records that should raise eyebrows concerns an unmarried young woman, Mary Teal, and wealthy tavern keeper, landowner and county sheriff Daniel Hand (Matthew Hand's unofficial father-in-law). In 1751, Daniel Hand married Hannah Page, who like Daniel was a descendant of one of the county's earliest families. Together they had seven children. Hannah Page Hand passed away in 1774, and Daniel Hand became a widower at the age of forty-four. His sons and eldest daughters by Hannah were of age at this time, but his youngest daughters were still minors. Within a year and a half, Daniel would become a father again, as suggested in "the King vs Mary Teel":

Cape May County Court of General Sessions & October Term 1775
The Grand Jurors for our Sovereign Lord the King upon their oaths &
affirmation do present that Mary Teel /Spinster/ of the Middle Precinct
of said County of Cape May on the first day of December in the year of
our Lord one Thousand seven Hundred and Seventy four in the fifteenth
year of the Reign of our Sovereign Lord George the Third King of great
Britain did at the Middle Precinct aforesaid in the County aforsd. Then
and there Fornication did Commit with some man to the Jurors aforesaid
unknown. To the evil example of all others & the peace of said Lord the
King his Crown & Dignity and against the Act of Assembly in such Case
made and provided.

At the October term in 1775, Mary Teal, described as "a spinster under the age of twenty one," was charged with fornication after bearing an illegitimate child. Mary refused to name the father of the child, and shortly before the Revolution began, at the January term of 1776, her father, John Teal, posted her bond of twenty pounds. While no record of a marriage for her has been found, she bore two more children.

Daniel Hand had been a widower for thirteen years when he died at the age of fifty-seven in 1787. In his lengthy will, he left all of his "Hand" sons and daughters plantations scattered throughout the county as well as "investment properties" in the form of valuable standing timber in the cedar swamps located in the northern part of the county. That is, with the exception of his son Daniel Hand Jr., who was to receive a small stipend of ten pounds annually to be doled out by Daniel Sr.'s son-in-law Nathaniel Holmes Sr. The family issues surrounding that bequest are unknown at this time.

In addition to listing the bequests to Daniel Hand's children by his wife, Hannah Page, the will then sheds light on the case of Mary Teal:

Item: I give to my son Jesse the son of Mary Teel my plantation in the
Middle Precint aforesaid at Horse Neck which I purchased of Elijah and
Shamgar Huet Together with all my Cedar Swamp Lying on the North East
Side of the Cedar Swamp Bridge....And Further it is my Will and I Soe
order that out of my Personal Estate be Raised the Sum of One Hundred
Pounds to Immediately when Raised Paid into the [hands] of my Trusty

Friend Phillip Hand for the Sole and Express Purpose of Bringing up and Educating my two Children, Jeremiah and Ezekiel Sons of Mary Teel and Soe appoint the said Phillip Hand and Nathaniel Holmes to be Guardians to take care of the persons and estates of the said Jeremiah and Ezekiel until they shall each come to the age of twenty years….And Further Soe Appoint Nathaniel Holmes to be the Guardian of my Said Son Jesse to take care of and Educate him until he shall be Twenty Years of age.

It was likely common knowledge who fathered Mary Teal's three sons, but at his death, Daniel Hand legally acknowledged his illegitimate sons and took care to provide for their future well-being. At the time of their father's death in 1787, Jesse, Jeremiah and Ezekiel were all underage, but Daniel didn't record their ages in his will. Daniel Hand's natural son Jesse was likely the eldest, as he was mentioned separately and inherited a plantation. If he was the child associated with Mary Teal's indictment in 1775, then Daniel was simply a middle-aged man having an illicit affair with a young woman who was less than half of his age. If Daniel Hand and Mary Teal began their relationship before his wife's death in 1774, then he was also an adulterer. While that possibility is pure speculation, it may shed light on the domestic issues that led to Daniel posting the following legal notice in the *Pennsylvania Journal* (Philadelphia) on October 4, 1770:

New Jersey, Cape May County, Oct. 4, 1770 Whereas Hannah, the wife of Daniel Hand, Esq; hath behaved herself in a very unbecoming manner and eloped from her said husband, on Thursday night last, without any provocation (supposed to have gone away with a certain Nathan Hand and Ezekiel Hand.) These are to forewarn all persons not to trust her on his account, as he will pay no debts of her contracting from the date hereof. Daniel Hand.

Hannah left her husband with the help of two of his cousins. (Ezekiel Hand owned a vessel trading between Cape May and Philadelphia.) Hannah Page Hand did return to her husband, as she died four years later and is buried next to Daniel and is surrounded by many of her children in the old Baptist Burial Ground in Cape May Court House.

Ironically, the most comprehensive Hand family history yet published, the *Hand Genealogy of Cape May County* (D. & Z. Hand), quotes parts of Daniel Hand's will but fails to mention his three "natural" sons by Mary

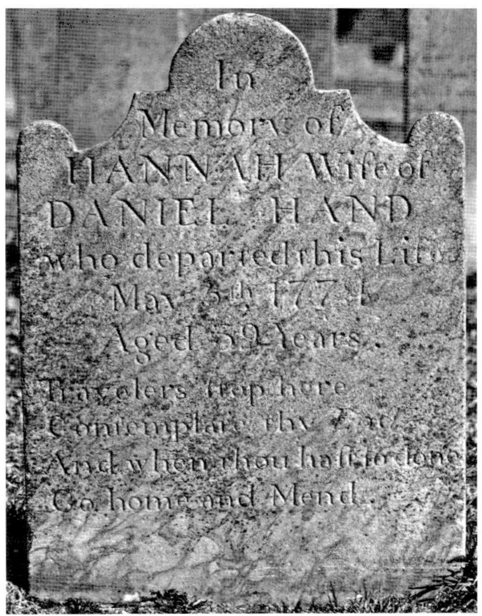
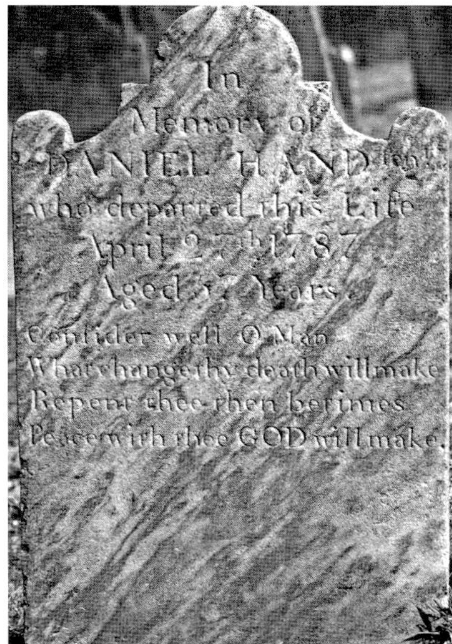

Left: The headstone of Hannah Page Hand, Baptist Burial Ground, Cape May Court House, New Jersey. *Photo by Jim Talone.*

Right: The headstone of Daniel Hand, Baptist Burial Ground, Cape May Court House, New Jersey. *Photo by Jim Talone.*

Teal. Dr. Zelophead Hand began compiling family history about 1857 up until his death in 1911, after which his brother Daniel continued the work and published a few copies in 1920. The brothers were direct descendants of Daniel Hand and apparently decided not to mention the long ago indiscretion of their ancestor.

TROUBLE NEXT DOOR

The justices of Cape May were fortunate in only having to deal with the aforementioned misbehavior of the county's citizens. In neighboring Cumberland and Gloucester Counties, the courts dealt with many of the same domestic disputes as in Cape May but also saw a surprising number of cases related to the Revolution itself. Dozens of residents of those two counties were charged with offenses ranging from "refusing the oath,

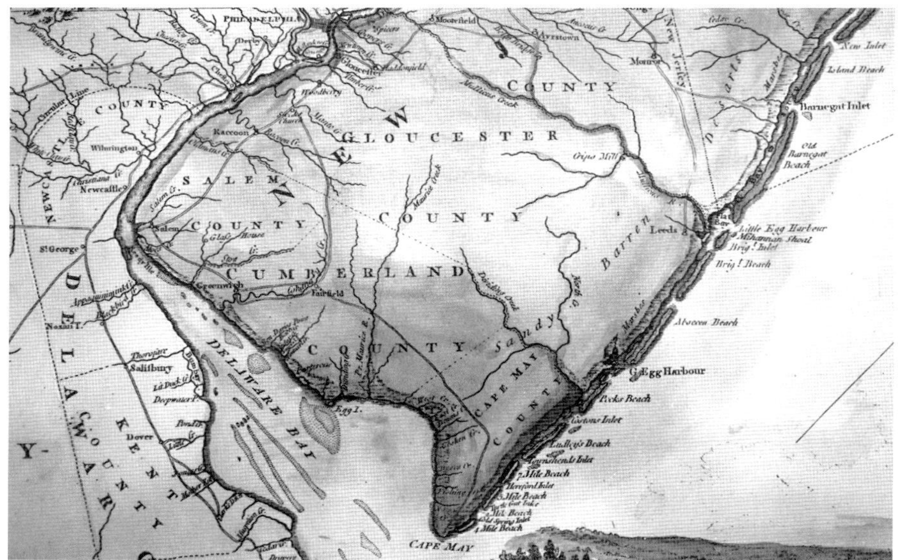

Holland-Pownall Map of Cape May and surrounding counties, 1776. *J.P. Hand collection.*

disaffection of government, going into the enemy's lines, and treason." One apparently unpatriotic mariner of Cumberland County, William Moore Jr., was charged with "Harbouring and Piloting the Enemy."

It is important to acknowledge the turmoil in the counties adjoining Cape May during the Revolution for a number of reasons. Foremost, a comparison of the court records of Cumberland County in particular illustrates just how unique Cape May County was in its support of the rebellion. Another reason for that comparison is the fact that to a certain degree, they were two similar communities reacting to the same political reality in different ways. It's important to note that quite a few of the families that were well established in Cumberland at this time had originally settled at Cape May a few generations earlier. Many more of Cumberland County's inhabitants had migrated from the same early settlements as had Cape May's oldest families—that is Eastern and Western Long Island, East Jersey and New England. The difference regarding the solidarity behind the fight for independence between the inhabitants of Cape May and the surrounding counties can be described as "as different as night and day."

Cape May had only two instances of land being confiscated for loyalty to the Crown, and in both cases, the land belonged to nonresidents. Over the

Obviously, some of the charges listed above were more serious than others. The offenses of treason and joining the enemy would seem to indicate that the men indicted held hardcore Tory sympathies. Those charged with going into the enemy's lines were likely motivated by financial gain, as was Silas Ireland, indicted for "counterfeiting continental currency." Many of those charged with disaffection to government may have been Tories or Tory sympathizers, or they might not have wanted to commit one way or the other. We can only guess as to why the Cumberland justices chose to charge two of Cape May's privateer captains, brothers James Willets Jr. and Enoch Willets, with the offense of horse racing. It may seem trivial to modern readers, especially when compared to the more serious criminal charges that were rampant during the war. James Willets was also a captain in the Cape May Militia, and he and his brother Enoch were the first cousins of Colonel Elijah Hand of the Cumberland Militia, who himself had been a justice in Cumberland County before the war.

THIRTY DOLLARS REWARD

RAN AWAY from the subscriber at Cape May, an APPRENTICE LAD fifteen years of age, a fresh complexion, light coloured hair. had on when he went away a light coloured jacket, striped wollen shirt, a pair of flannel trowsers, he carried away two new shirts of his Master's. Whoever takes up said ran away, and secures him so that his Master may have him again, shall have the above reward and reasonable charges paid, by
DARIUS CORSON.

Cape May privateer Darius Corson posted this legal notice in an attempt to retrieve his unnamed runaway apprentice, *Pennsylvania Packet*, June 13, 1780. *Courtesy of the American Antiquarian Society.*

By 1751, roughly a half century after permanent European settlement, there were twenty-five slaves living among the county's 246 households. Broken down further, there were ten slaves in the Lower Precinct, thirteen slaves in the Middle Precinct and only two slaves held in the predominately Quaker Upper Precinct. Just prior to the Revolution, the tax rolls for the year 1774 show a gradual increase to a total of thirty-nine slaves countywide—Lower Precinct, eight slaves; Middle Precinct, seventeen slaves; Upper Precinct, fourteen slaves. The increase in slave ownership in the Quaker-dominated Upper Precinct may be attributed to non-Quaker families moving into the area as well as a large number of members of the Society of Friends being read out of meeting for various infractions.

The tax rolls for 1784, the year after the war ended, clearly show a marked rise in slave ownership in Cape May County. In one decade, the number of slaves held in the county more than doubled to a total of 104 slaves. While the number of slaves held in the sparsely populated Upper Precinct actually dropped to 9, the number of slaves more than tripled in the Lower and Middle Precincts to 33 and 62, respectively. Two possible factors may have contributed to the spike in slave ownership at Cape May during the war. It can be speculated that the enormous sums of money made in successful privateer cruises enabled some county residents who previously couldn't afford such a luxury, to purchase slaves with the profits of those cruises.

According to contemporary newspaper accounts, some of those same Cape May privateers captured prize vessels that had slaves on board. Published legal notices of the time reveal that slaves on board captured prizes were often sold at vendue (public auction) along with the cargoes, armaments and the vessels themselves.

A number of Cape May privateer captains and others associated with the trade are listed as slave owners on the 1784 tax list. Many were first-time slave owners and most owned one slave, including privateer captains

TO be fold at publick vendue on Thurfday the 2d of December next, at Samuel Cooper's Ferry, oppofite Philadelphia, at three o'clock, Five very likely young NEGRO LADS, from 15 to 20 years of age, taken in the prize brig Triton.
By order of the Court of Admiralty,
JOS. POTTS, Marfhal.
New-Jerfey, November 22, 1779.   1w‡

Runaway slaves on board captured British prizes were either claimed by their owners or sold along with the vessel and cargo, *New-Jersey Gazette*, November 24, 1779. *Courtesy of the American Antiquarian Society.*

Moses Griffing, Joseph Edwards, John Golden, James Willets Jr. and Colonel Nicholas Stillwell and privateer lieutenants Israel Stites and John Teal. Others who had owned one slave before the war, but by 1784 had increased the number of slaves owned included privateer captains Lieutenant Colonel Enoch Stillwell (four), Colonel Elijah Hand (three) and his brother Assemblyman Jonathan Hand Esq. (three). Add to that list privateer investors and owners Thomas Leaming Esq. (five), Jesse Hand (six) and merchant George Taylor Sr. (six).

Both before and after the war, the largest slaveholders in the county were the Leamings and Hands of the Middle Precinct and the Hughes family of the Lower Precinct. In 1784, various members of the Hughes family held twelve slaves; at the time of his death in 1812, wealthy tavern keeper Memucan Hughes owned that many himself.

The Revolutionary War–era increase in slave ownership at Cape May didn't last long. Within a few decades, the county's slave owners began to manumit their slaves, as court records show a steady flow of slave manumissions leading up to the last manumission in 1835. After that date, no African American was held in bondage in Cape May County. Whether by coincidence or not, the steady manumission of slaves in the county paralleled the rise of the Methodist Episcopal Church at Cape May. Interestingly, many if not most of the county's ex-slaves continued to work for their former masters, no longer as slaves but as employees working for wages and board. In the case of elderly ex-slaves in Cape May County, many were cared for and lived out their lives with the families that had previously owned them.

To whom it may concern.

State of New-Jersey, to wit.

NOTICE is hereby given, that a court of admiralty will be held at the house of James Eldail, in Burlington, on Wednesday the 26th day of June next, at the hour of ten in the forenoon of the same day, then and there to try the truth of the facts alledged in the bill of Hope Willets, commander of the armed boat Black Joke; and Joseph Edwards, commander of the armed boat Luck and Fortune, who as well, &c. against a certain sloop or vessel called the Nancy, which lately failed from Maurice River in the said state, laden with lumber and tar, was captured at sea by the Fair American, a British cruizer, commanded by William Nelson; and afterwards re-captured by the said Captains, Willets and Edwards, together with her tackle, apparel, furniture and cargo, and two Negro slaves, named Obadiah Gale, and Edward Carter; to the end and intent that the owner or owners of the said vessel, or any other person or persons interested therein, may appear and shew cause, if any they have, why the said vessel, with her tackle, apparel, furniture, cargo and said Negro slaves, should not be condemned to the captors thereof, and a decree thereon pass, pursuant to the prayer of the said bill.

By order of the Judge,
JOSEPH BLOOMFIELD, Reg.

Burlington, May 29, 1782.   3w

To all whom it may concern.

New-Jersey ss.

NOTICE is hereby given, that a court of admiralty will be held at the court house in Burlington, on Monday the 22d day of November next, at ten o'clock in the forenoon of the same day, then and there to try the truth of the facts alledged in the bills of Rufus Gardner and Stephen Decatur, (who as well, &c.) against the schooner or vessel called the Hope; and also of Yelverton Taylor and Stephen Decatur, (who as well, &c.) against the brigantine or vessel called the Triton, lately commanded by Jonathan Cooper, and the following negro slaves, found on board the said brigantine at the time of her capture, to wit, Jack, Harry, Sam, James, Anthony and Jack; to the end and intent, that the owner or owners of the said vessels and negro slaves, or any person or persons concerned therein, may appear, and shew cause, if any they have, why the said vessels, negro slaves and cargoes, should not be condemned, according to the prayers of the said bills.

By order of the Judge,

Left: Legal notice regarding the recapture of the sloop *Nancy* by Hope Willets and Joseph Edwards of Cape May, *New-Jersey Gazette*, June 2, 1782. *Courtesy of the American Antiquarian Society.*

Right: Legal notice regarding the prize brig *Triton*, cargo and slaves found on board, *New-Jersey Gazette*, October 27, 1779. *Courtesy of the American Antiquarian Society.*

In one notable instance, Nathaniel Holmes Sr. directed in his will that an interest-bearing trust fund be established for "the loving care and keeping" of Viney, an elderly ex-slave who lived in his household. The principal of that fund, $800, was a small fortune in 1834. In addition to the interest in cash paid to her daughter, Rhuma Scott, annually, the endowment allowed for salt hay to feed one cow for as long as Viney should live. Holmes was a young privateer crewman during the Revolution and after the war went on to become a prominent merchant, landowner and major in the Cape May Militia during the Whiskey Rebellion. He was also the younger brother of privateer investor John Holmes Sr. and the son-in-law of Daniel Hand Sr., the Revolutionary War–era county sheriff, wealthy landowner and tavern keeper, both of whom are mentioned in chapter 3.

And lastly, in a tale that seems to have jumped from the pages of a Mark Twain novel, we have the story of two runaways—a thirty-two-year-old slave and a white apprentice boy of seventeen—and a stolen boat. On July 14, 1784, Jonathan Hand Esq., who had been a member of the New Jersey Assembly before and during the war and was the brother of privateer captain Colonel Elijah Hand, posted the following legal notice in Benjamin Franklin's *Pennsylvania Gazette*:

FIVE POUNDS Reward

Run away in the night of the 7th of June inst. From the subscriber, living in Cape-May county, and state of New-Jersey, a Negroe Man Slave, and a white apprentice Lad. The Negroe, named Nero, 32 years of age, 5 feet 8 or 9 inches high pretty lusty and well set, bold and subtle, has large eyes, a flatish nose, and a trembling in his hands when he does anything that requires steadiness; had on a new grey homespun jacket of fulled cloth, made sailor fashion without skirts, but round close cuffs, and carved pewter buttons; new thickset trousers, the same of the jacket, an old castor [beaver] hat, and a pair of large thick shoes much worn....The apprentice named Aaron Hand, 17 years of age, about 5 feet 6 or 7 inches high, slender built, brown complexion, pretty large black eyes and black strait hair; had on a new grey homespun jacket and trowsers made of thick cloth, the jacket cut sailor fashion, with flat metal buttons, homespun linen shirt, felt hat, old shoes, and square silver buckles....As they had a boat, it is likely they would try to get on board some outward bound vessel, or go over into Delaware state, and endeavor to push for the new country, as it is thought the Negroe has a sham pass, and will endeavor to pass as free; it is also expected that one or both of them will change their names, especially the Negroe. Whoever takes up and secures said Negroe and apprentice, so as their master may get them again (or the Negroe only, in case the lad cannot be found) shall have the above reward, and reasonable charges, paid by JONATHAN HAND. N.B. All masters of vessels are forewarned not to carry them off.
June 10. 1784.

In addition to the clothes on their backs, the pair of runaways also pilfered as much additional clothing as they could carry from their master's house. The young apprentice, Aaron Hand, was surely a relative of Jonathan Hand Esq. and may have been the son of his late brother, Recompence Hand, of Dividing Creek, Cumberland County. Whether they were apprehended after making their escape or returned to their master voluntarily may never be known. What is known is that Nero did return to the county and was freed from bondage at some point and lived to the relatively advanced age of sixty-four. His will may be the only one recorded from Cape May County to a resident with only one name (the surname Emmerson was added to the document after the fact):

be. Griffing and four men took *George* into Egg Harbor, but the ship's papers were not to be found. As the wind had been from the southwest, *George* could have shipped easily to New York but entered Egg Harbor. The crew did not know that Philadelphia had been evacuated by the British. Crawford claimed they were headed for Egg Harbor, not New York, since they had left the Scottish boat.

John Wood

Wood joined the ship in St. Kitts and was told by Captain Smith that they were headed for New York, Philadelphia or somewhere thereabout. They sailed with a British convoy of warships headed for New York, and Wood alleged that Captain Smith said he was afraid of English privateers. According to Wood, the papers were burned by the mate after a schooner hailed them. Included were signal instructions. The ship may have been owned by Moor and Johnson of St. Kitts since the pay vouchers were drawn on their account. Some of these papers were produced by Moses Griffing.

The first land sighted was probably Cape May, but they were headed for Egg Harbor. Wood confirmed Crawford's assertion that the wind was strong from the southwest but the captain did not intend to go to New York. He also testified that he was offered one hundred pounds by Captain Griffing in the presence of Lieutenant Stillwell to give evidence in favor of condemning the *George*.

Peter Morris

Morland, a mate, and Smith told Morris they were bound for Egg Harbor loaded with rum. He had heard no mention of ship's papers but overhead the captain say they were bound for Egg Harbor. The wind from south–southwest would have made it easier to go to New York than into Egg Harbor. Morris insisted the *George*, which was leaking, had no intention of going to Philadelphia. The mate wanted an American pilot, but the schooner flying Continental colors boarded the *George*.

James Robinson

Robinson was a sailor on British privateers, who shipped on board the *George* and believed they were headed for New York. *George* lost its bowsprit and sheathing and wanted to put in to Egg Harbor. Robinson believed the ship had been captured by a pilot.

Lewis Augustus Ward

Ward wanted passage to America to join the U.S. Army, and he spoke with Morland and Smith, who said they were headed to an American-friendly port. He was later told in confidence that they were headed to Little Egg Harbor. Captain Smith wanted silence on this since he was afraid the men would take the ship. Second Mate Palmer also told Ward the *George* was not headed for New York. Ward told the mate they were headed for Egg Harbor, and they began to clean the blunderbusses for a mutiny.

Richard Stockton, lawyer for the defendant, called Captain Robert Smith, who claimed the ship was not British but owned by Jennings, a Dutchman from St. Eustatius. It was headed for a port controlled by Americans, Philadelphia. A bill of lading from the *George* was produced, indicating the cargo was bound for Mr. Anderson and Caldwell of Philadelphia and sent by Mr. Jennings of St. Eustatius. Caldwell produced a letter stating the *George*'s cargo, £1,268.16 of rum, was for him. But papers were not found on the *George* to corroborate this. Griffing attested that there were no papers on the *George*—Smith claimed he had hidden the papers.

Despite all this rather ambiguous testimony, the jury verdict came down on October 30, 1778, that the sloop *George* and all its cargo were to be condemned as a prize and be sold for the benefit of Moses Griffing.

However, this verdict was overturned on appeal in the federal appeals court on December 23, 1780. In the end, the owner from St. Eustatius, Jennings, won.

After the American Revolution, Sarah and Moses Griffing settled in Cape May County in the Middle Precinct. In the 1784 tax rolls he is listed as householder with nine family members and one slave but no land. Moses's family Bible indicates he was captured during the war and imprisoned on the infamous *New Jersey* with many other Cape May privateers. Sarah Griffing petitioned General Washington to have her husband released, and according to Collins, Johnston never said injurious things about America and was a friend to the cause.

Witness Captain Evan Walborne

Walborne had known Johnston for sixteen to seventeen years and knew he owned two dwellings in Newport, including a still house and bake house. Friendly to the United States, Johnston was even appointed by a Mr. Shaw with a flag of truce to go from Newport to New London.

Witness John Martin

The resident of Cape Cod met Johnston and the *Fame* in Port San Antonio in Jamaica. Johnston was shipping salt, beef and other goods from there to Matthews Bay in Jamaica. Martin heard him say he was concerned about American privateers operating off Jamaica.

Martin sailed with the *Fame* and six ships of war in the fleet and heard Johnston say they were bound for New York but would go to Nantucket or Rhode Island later. After arriving, *Fame* ran down to the Delaware Bay and sought a pilot. A boat told the crew that the British had quit Philadelphia and told Johnston he must fight. The other ship was a brig of fourteen guns.

The brig gave the *Fame* water and told the captain to keep away from shore where the American privateers hid out. Heading north from Cape May, a fast sloop bore down on the *Fame*. Yelverton Taylor on the *Comet* fired at the *Fame*.

Witness Mate Simeon Swaine of the Fame

Mate Swaine on the *Fame* gave much the same testimony as the earlier character witnesses and Martin, who was on board at the time of the capture. After making land north of Cape May, *Fame* encountered a vessel, but the other ship did not know if the British still held Philadelphia. Captain Johnston asked for water and planned to go up the Delaware but had no knowledge of the river. The crew was warned of privateers cruising Egg Harbor, but despite keeping off the land and adding more sail, they were shot at by what they had thought was an English ship. Swaine claimed to have advised striking the colors because they could not outrun or defend against the privateer. Under cross-examination, Swaine admitted that there was no mention of going to an American port until the ship was in distress and in need of sail and water.

The jury deliberated until January 14, 1779, and the judge declared the *Fame* condemned and sold at public vendue, trial costs to be paid from sale of the ship and cargo.

Samuel Johnston immediately filed an appeal, but it was decided against the claimants in 1780.

There are a handful more of cases like these three above. The stories are all similar. A merchantman leaves the Caribbean bound for ports in the colonies but never clearly admits whether the destination is American or British controlled. Usually, the ship's papers were thrown overboard or burned when they were chased by privateers. Juries in the New Jersey courts may have not been entirely impartial since claimants were usually rebuffed and the privateer captains and owners awarded the prizes.

St Eustatius—The Small but Crucial Island to the American Cause

A major exception to the events described in the aforementioned is the fact that ships leaving from Oraniestaat, St. Eustatius, a Dutch colony, were often directly headed to colonial ports for the benefit of the American cause. In fact, some historians believe that nearly one-half of all supplies transshipped from Europe, especially from Spain, France and the Netherlands, to America came through this tiny Dutch island. In fact, the island was dubbed the "Golden Rock." A very large number of the Eustatian merchants were Jews who had emigrated from Europe and South America.

On November 16, 1776, the American brig *Andrew Doria* sailed into Port Orange from its home port in Gloucester City, New Jersey, and fired a thirteen-gun salute that was returned with the regulation nine- or eleven-gun retort from the fort. This event marked the first international recognition of the fledgling United States and was the famous "First Salute" memorialized in Barbara Tuchman's *The First Salute*, a historical treatise of the Revolution.

befell quite a few of the other Cape May privateer captains, including Elijah Hand's second cousin Enoch Stillwell and Stillwell's brother-in-law, Moses Griffing. Fortunately for these men and their crews, the efforts of another distant cousin, Thomas Leaming Jr., resulted in their being exchanged for British and Hessian prisoners held by the Americans.

Almost fifty years after the end of the war (June 7, 1832), Congress passed an act authorizing pensions for the relatively few remaining veterans of the Revolution. These aging veterans, who were mere boys during the conflict, included Cape May County natives Recompence Hand, Henry Iszard, Jeremiah Hand, Nathaniel Holmes Sr. and others.

After the war, Colonel Elijah Hand and his wife, Rachel, retired to their plantation at Cape May. In 1789, just six years after his last wartime service, Elijah died intestate—that is, without a will—at the age of sixty. Rachel died in 1795, leaving behind their three children and thirteen grandchildren. At the present time, there are thousands of the descendants of this couple living in South Jersey and throughout the United States.

10

NAVAL BATTLES IN AND AROUND CAPE MAY

D.P. STITES

THERE ARE NUMEROUS ACCOUNTS THAT indicate there were no naval battles in the American Revolution near Cape May. The one exception is the Battle of Turtle Gut Inlet (described in more detail later). Our research has shown another much more important action took place in 1782 right off Cape May Point in the inlet of the Delaware between the British sloop *General Monk* and an American privateer, the *HyderAlly*, captained by the famous American naval hero Captain Joshua Barney.

The Battle of Turtle Gut Inlet, a relatively minor engagement, took place on July 29, 1776 , in Turtle Gut Inlet—now closed in with sand near Wildwood Crest. The well-known American captain John Barry was the master of the USS *Lexington*. Robert Morris had commissioned a privateer brig, *Nancy*, attempt to run the British blockade of the Delaware. Morris shipped from the Caribbean with a load of gunpowder, guns and rum for the Port of Philadelphia. Barry and the *Lexington*, a 14-gun sloop, were sent out to accompany *Nancy* and soon joined by the 198-gun *Reprisal*, captained by Lambert Wickes; and the 8-gun *Wasp*, captained by William Hallock. The British blockade forces were led by HMS *Liverpool*, a 28-gun ship captained by Henry Bellew; the 32-gun HMS *Orpheus*, captained by Charles Hudson; and the 16-gun *Kingfisher*, captained by Alexander Graeme.

On June 28, the American blockade runner *Nancy* was spotted heading for the Delaware Bay inlet, and Barry, on the *Lexington*, was signaled for help. He contacted the remaining American ships in the area, and the *Nancy*

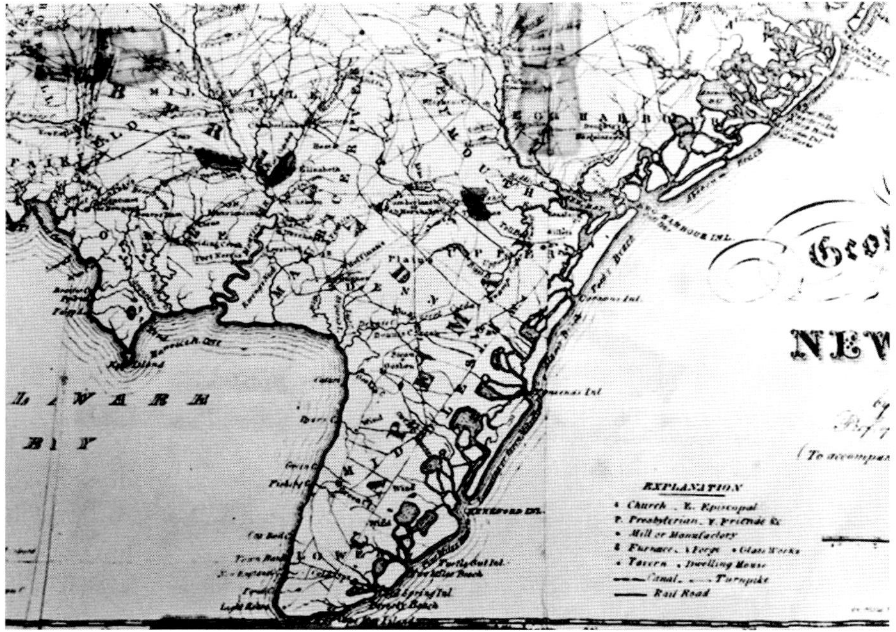

Portion of Rogers' Map, South Jersey, 1839. *J.P. Hand collection.*

headed for refuge into Turtle Gut Inlet. On the 29, it ran aground in a heavy fog. The British vessels were unable to pursue in the shallow waters of the inland waterway but continued to shell *Nancy* from offshore. Barry and the other captains and crews attempted to offload the cargo from the grounded *Nancy*. They succeeded in rowing more than 250 kegs of gunpowder to the shore in the ship's longboats. The British bombardment heavily damaged the *Nancy*. However, Barry rigged a giant fuse using the sail and, with 100 kegs of gunpowder still in the hold, deceived the British by lowering her flag. After the British boarded the *Nancy*, the powder was ignited, resulting in a significant number of British casualties. Lieutenant Richard Wickes, the brother of the American captain Lambert Wickes, was a casualty, and he was interred at Cold Spring Cemetery.

Despite the interest in the Turtle Gut Bay incident, a much larger and more important battle occurred at the mouth of the Delaware right off Cape May Island on April 8, 1782, between the American naval sloop *Hyder Ally* and the British sloop *General Monk*. The *Hyder Ally*, actually a privateer letter of marque, was commanded by the youthful Lieutenant Joshua Barney, one of the founders of the American navy.

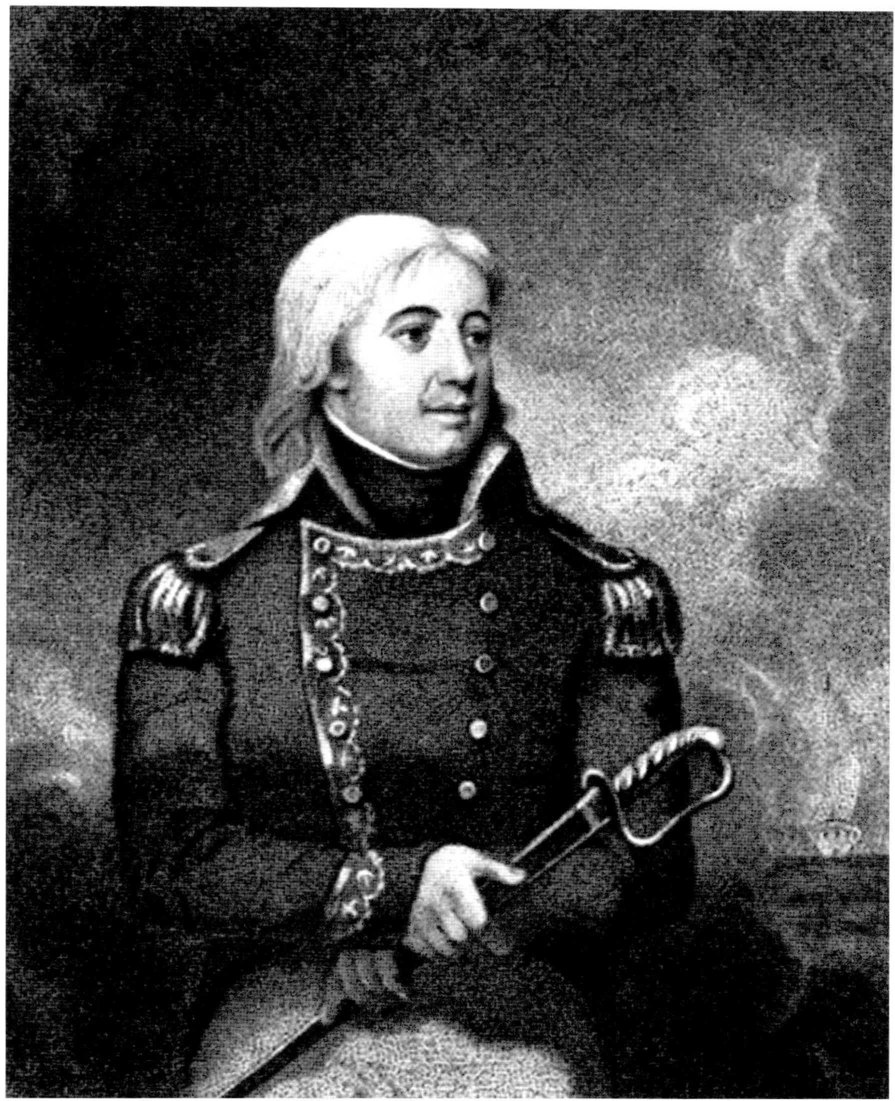

Joshua Barney. *University of Pittsburgh Library.*

Joshua Barney was born near Baltimore, Maryland, on July 6, 1759. His parents were prosperous land owners. He was raised with thirteen siblings near the settlement of Bear Creek on the Patapsco Neck and quit school at the age of ten, expressing an interest in going to sea. After working in a counting house for about a year, Barney quit and signed on as hand aboard

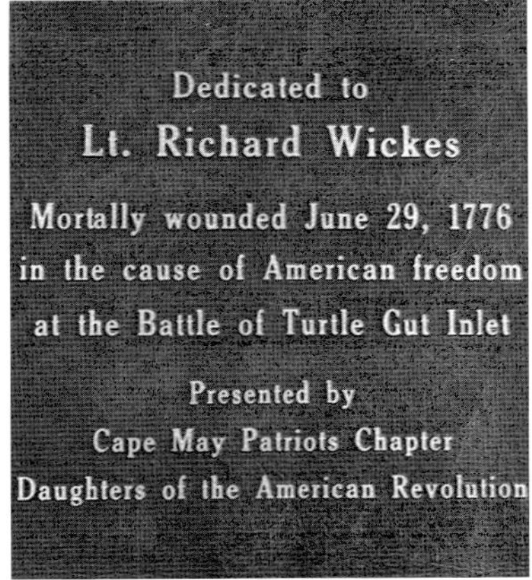

Richard Wickes plaque, Cold Spring Cemetery, New Jersey. *Photo by Jim Talone.*

the schooner *Chesapeake*. Soon after his father died in a farming accident, he joined his brother-in-law Captain Thomas Drysdale, the master of a small brig, the *Sidney*. In December 1774, the fifteen-year-old Barney set sail from Baltimore on the *Sidney* with a cargo of wheat bound for Nice, France. While crossing the Atlantic Ocean, Drysdale died of a fever, and the young Barney found himself in command of the brig. Despite bad weather and damage to the ship, he managed to put in at Gibraltar for repairs. The trip ended successfully in Nice, and the cargo sold at a profit. After a brief interlude in which Barney was commandeered by Spain to transport troops, he sailed home with a rich cargo. The owners of the ship were suitably impressed with the mere boy captain.

Barney underwent a series of American naval appointments after the Continental Congress established the American navy in 1775. At sixteen, he accepted the position of master mate aboard the sloop *Hornet* but was later transferred to the *Wasp*. Joshua Barney was commissioned a lieutenant in 1776 and served aboard the sloop *Sachem*, which encountered a British merchant brig bound for New York. After a spirited battle between the two ships, *Sachem*'s captain was wounded, and Barney assumed command. A victory for the Americans ensued, and the British ship was brought into Philadelphia as a war prize. Next, he was assigned to the American eleven-gun ship the *Andrew Doria*. Barney was eventually captured by the British at sea but later paroled and exchanged for an officer of similar rank in the British navy. He was briefly captured again and spent time on a British prison ship, the *St. Albans*. After recuperating, he served aboard the brig *Saratoga* but was recaptured and sent to the notorious Old Mill Prison in England. After a daring escape, which he managed by concealing himself in a phony British uniform, Joshua Barney slipped off to France, where he met Benjamin Franklin and John Paul Jones. He eventually made his way back to Philadelphia via Holland and resumed his naval duties as commander of a privateer, the *HyderAlly*.

Throughout the American Revolution, naval blockades of important waterways to the sea were tactics used by both sides of the conflict. The

British abandoned the occupation of Philadelphia after less than one year in 1777 in response to the French joining the Rebels' side. However, to prevent trade with the colonies' largest port in Philadelphia, a constant patrol of British warships and Loyalist privateers outfitted in New York blockaded the mouth of the Delaware and plied the waterways up and down the river to harass Rebel shipping. In 1780, in a direct response to these threats, a group of private citizens and merchants in Philadelphia convinced the Pennsylvania assembly to appropriate £25,000 to build and equip or purchase warships to counter these harassments. In 1782, Lieutenant Joshua Barney, after returning from his captivity in Europe, was given command of a sloop, the *HyderAlly*, which was actually a private vessel owned by John Willcocks. Barney was merely twenty-three at the time. The *HyderAlly* was equipped with sixteen six-pounders and a crew of about 110 men and officers. It was named for Hyder Ali, the ruler of the Kingdom of Mysore in India and an enemy of the British. Barney's command also included privateer sloops, the ten-gun *Charming Sally* and the twelve-gun *General Greene*. They were to escort five merchantmen from Philadelphia to the mouth of the Delaware in early April 1782.

Barney's main adversary in the impeding action was the twenty-four-gun sloop *General Monk*, commanded by Captain Josiah Rogers. The *General Monk* was previously known as the *General Washington*, an American privateer captured by the British at the Battle of Charleston, South Carolina.

The description that follows is based largely on the diary of Joshua Barney himself. On the evening of April 7, 1782, Rogers was cruising off Cape Henlopen with a frigate, the *Quebec*, commanded by a Captain Mason. In Cape May roads, they encountered eight enemy vessels and anchored, waiting to attack in the morning. Rogers proceeded up the river and was joined by a British privateer, the captured *Fair American*. At noon, the American force of eight vessels discovered them rounding Cape May Point. Rogers in the *General Monk* immediately attacked, and an American vessel of twelve guns immediately struck its colors. Another American vessel of the same size ran aground and was abandoned by the crew, but several others sailed to safety up the Maurice River. The British *Fair American* ran aground. Rogers then approached the *HyderAlly*, which was bristling with men and guns, but he was reluctant to attack, since most of the British guns were carronades not cannons. The carronades could cause severe damage to adversaries but only at relatively close range. Barney then sailed abreast of the *Monk*, readying a broadside, but waited until the last minute to open his gun ports. In another daring ruse, he purposely and incorrectly signaled a turn aport but actually turned to the starboard, throwing the *Monk*'s gunners into confusion. This resulted in a collision, and the two vessels were entangled. Barney's men fired grapeshot, muskets and other small arms into the nearby *Monk*'s decks—totally devastating the British crew.

The American ship made fast work of the British sloop, firing thirteen broadsides in the ensuing twenty-six minutes. Buck's County (Pennsylvania) riflemen fired into the *Monk*'s decks from the topsail perches on the *HyderAlly* with devastating accuracy. Captain Rogers was wounded in the foot and lost his first lieutenant, purser, surgeon, boatswain and chief gunner—26 of 136 British crewmen were killed and 33 men wounded. A midshipman bravely struck *General Monk*'s colors after only twenty-six minutes of fighting. The *HyderAlly* had only 4 killed and 11 wounded. The frigate *Quebec* quit the scene, running away to the safety of the Atlantic Ocean.

The prize, *General Monk*, was hastily fitted out for sailing and navigated up the Delaware, where it was greeted by a huge Philadelphia crowd. Captain Rogers was taken prisoner and well treated in the home of Quakers. On April 13, the Pennsylvania legislature proclaimed resolutions congratulating Lieutenant Barney and striking a very expensive sword to honor him. The sword, which was presented to Barney by Governor Dickinson, is still in the Daughters of the American Revolution museum in Washington, D.C. Barney later commissioned a portrait of the Battle of the Delaware while serving in France. The portrait, by artist Louis-Phillipe Crepin, hangs in the Naval Academy Museum at Annapolis, Maryland. Barney went on to eventually become a naval hero of the War of 1812. He died in 1818 from a serious wound contracted at the Battle of Bladensburg.

An interesting footnote comes from the 1850 U.S. Census of Cape May County, New Jersey, where a ninety-seven-year-old black man, Beny Dinah, comments that he saw the battle between the *HyderAlly* and the *General Monk* many years earlier.

This is the affidavit filed in a Philadelphia court by a Cape May man, Ezekiel Hand Teel, who was a fourteen-year-old crewman on board the *HyderAlly* during the battle:

Affidavit of Ezekiel Hand Teel Nov 14, 1832 [From National Archives Application for Revolutionary War Pensions]

City of Philadelphia
State of Pennsylvania
On this 14ᵗʰ day of November 1832, personally Appeared in Open Court,

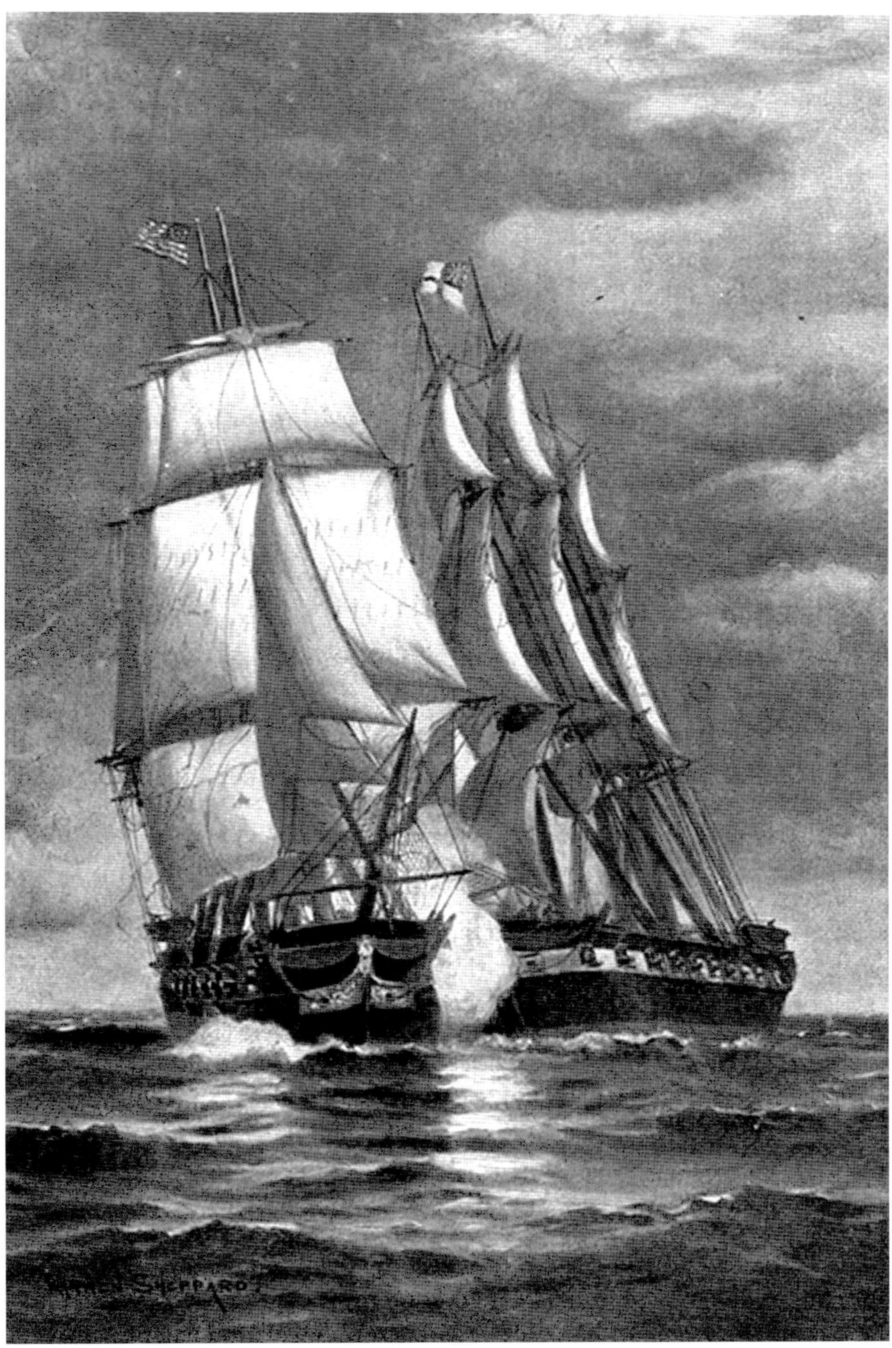

HyderAlly and *Monk. U.S. Navy Art Collection.*

Before the Court of Comm. Pleas now sitting, Ezekiel H. Teel a resident of Philadelphia State of Pennsylvania, Aged 63 years past. Who being first duly sworn according to Law, Doth on his oath make the following Declaration, in order to Obtain the benefit of the act of Congress, passed the Seventh of June 1832.

I was born in the County of Cape May, New Jersey Entered on board the Ship Hyder-Alley, *Commanded by Capt. Barney. 1ˢᵗ Officer Lt. Starr 2nd Lt. Matherson. J. Edwards assistant Surgeon. Sailed from the port of Philadelphia Down the Delaware on a Cruise, and our station on the Bay in the month of April. On our way down was met by the British Ship* General Monk *just from New York. We met, the action commenced past meridian [midday], and after severe Action which lasted 35 Minutes, we took her and sent her up to the City. We then repaired at Chester, and after refitting returned to our Cruising Ground. in a few days after, we fell in with a British Pilot boat Schooner Near the Capes. Called the* Hookem *we Took her and sent her in to the port Of Philadelphia. I was in actual service near six months. I then entered On board the Tender, a Sloop called the* Harlequin, *Tender to the* Hyder Alley *I was*
Five months in service on board this vessel, our Capt. was Enoch Stillwell, 1ˢᵗ Liunt. Nathaniel Holmes. Sometime after I entered on board a Gunboat, belonged to the State of N. Jersey called the State boat. Capt. Elijah Hand, did duty on Board of her for some months. I was in the 14ᵗʰ year of my age when first I entered Into service. Continued as above stated in the service of my Country. Have no discharge or papers, have never received any pension from the State or United States and now rest my claim in this county of my country.
Ezekiel H Teel
Sworn and Subscribed the
Day and Year aforesaid—
F.A. Raybold

Common Pleas
Personally appeared in Open Court, before the Court of Sessions Joshua Edwards Assistant Surgeon on board the Ship Hyder Alley *at the time and on the cruise when she captured the* General Monk. *Who being duly Sworn according to Law, Doth declare and say; that he is fully satisfied and Believes that, Ezekiel H. Teel the above applicant was on board the said Ship under The command of Capt. Barney and until sometime after*

the Action with The General Monk when he was detached to the Tender,
of the Hyder Alley, *and As I understand and fully believe, and that he*
served out the residue Of the period under Capt. Barney and Capt. Starr
until the early Part of October in 1782. And that full credit may be given
to his declaration as within stated.
Js Edwards

Reproduced by permission of the United States Naval Academy Museum, Annapolis, Maryland, this painting was commissioned by Joshua Barney in France in 1802 and rendered by the French painter Louis-Phillipe Crepin.

Several contemporary newspaper articles chronicle two interesting facts about the *General Monk*. In the *Pennsylvania Packet* of April 18, 1782 a notice stated:

On Wednesday Next (the 24ᵗʰ instant , April) at XII o'Clock Noon at the
COFFEE HOUSE; Will be sold at public auction, The Ship General

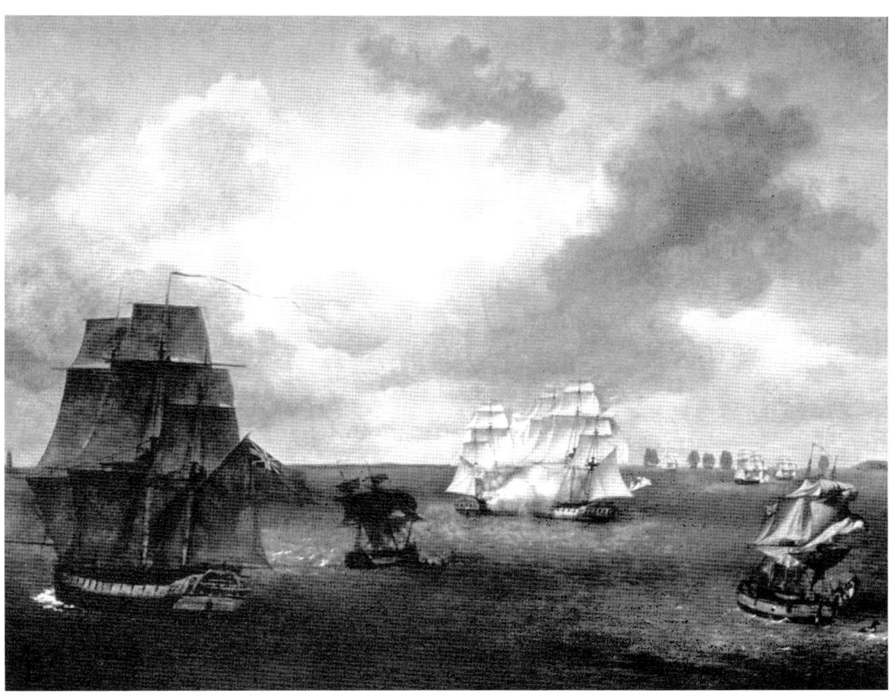

HyderAlly and *Monk* Battle in Delaware. *U.S. Naval Academy Museum, Annapolis, Maryland.*

Monk, With all her Guns, Tackle, Apparel and Furniture agreeable to an inventory to be seen at the place of sale, being a Sloop of War, formerly in the service of the King of Great-Britain and captured by the Ship HYDER ALLY, *commanded by Joshua Barney, esq. By Order of the Court of Admiralty Clement Biddle, Marshal. April 17.*

In that same newspaper edition, the *Pennsylvania Packet* offered the following news item:

The ship General Monk *shewed 24 guns, 6 of which were wood and the remainder nine-pounders. The* Hyder Ally *had 4 nines and 12 fixes. The action lasted about 28 minutes, in which time the* Monk *had 20 men killed and 33 wounded, and the* Hyder Ally *3 killed and 11 wounded. We do not recall a single instance, before this of a king's ship carrying wooden guns.*

11

CAPTAIN ENOCH STILLWELL AND THE *HAWK*

J.P. HAND

Delaware Bay Pilot turned privateer captain Yelverton Taylor can be considered the most successful of the privateers operating out of the Delaware Bay. Taylor may not have captured the most prizes, that distinction likely belongs to Cape May County's John Goldin, who, according to one contemporary Philadelphia newspaper account, took nineteen prizes as commander of the *Skunk*, an open boat with two guns and a crew of seventeen. Captain Taylor did capture at least twelve prizes of substance—that is, prizes that were valuable enough to be advertised for auction in the papers of Philadelphia and nearby Trenton, New Jersey.

Among those twelve vessels taken by Yelverton Taylor and his men was the brig *Triton*, a prize that may have been the most important one captured by the region's privateers in regard to its effect on the war effort. More important than the vessel itself was the "cargo" of over 125 officers and men of a Hessian regiment who were eventually exchanged for American privateers and soldiers held in the notorious prison ships of New York (see chapter 5).

Perhaps the most financially valuable prize taken by the Cape May privateers during the American Revolution was the dual capture of the brig *Lyon* and the schooner *Henry* by Captain Enoch Stillwell, master of the privateer schooner *Hawk*. The *Hawk* mounted ten guns and sailed with a crew of fifty. The vessel was owned by a group of investors, including Cape May's Thomas Leaming Jr., Jesse Hand and others (such as the captain,

P H I L A D E L P H I A, June 17.

An open boat, called the Skunk, mounting two guns, and 17 men, belonging to Egg-harbour, fent in there laft Wednefday a veffel with a valuable cargo, which makes her nineteenth prize fince fhe was fitted out.

A Boston paper reported the nineteen prizes taken by the *Skunk*, a small privateer vessel from Cape May, *Independent Chronicle*, July 8, 1779. *Courtesy of the American Antiquarian Society.*

possibly his brother Colonel Nicholas Stillwell and brother-in-law Colonel Richard Somers). The capture of the *Lyon* (also referred to as the *Lion* or *Leportax*) was reported in the *Pennsylvania Journal* or *Weekly Advertiser* of September 8, 1779:

> *Jamaica the first of August last. The schooner* Hawk, *Capt. Stillwell, last week conducted into Morris's* [Maurice] *River the brig* Lyon, *Capt. Child, from Jamaica for New York, with 203 hogsheads of rum—This is the fourth cargo that has fallen into our hands out of the fleet that sailed from.*

The schooner *Henry*, apparently taken in the same encounter by Enoch Stillwell and his crew, was advertised for sale at the bay front plantation of Enoch's brother Colonel Nicholas Stillwell Jr. as posted in the *New-Jersey Gazette* of September 8, 1779. Note that the description of the cargo would suggest that the vessel was from the same fleet as the *Lyon*:

> *New-Jersey, September 4, 1779*
> *To be sold at Public Vendue, at the Forks of Little Egg-Harbour, on Thursday the 19th inst.* [instant] *The Sloop* RECOVERY, *a fine vessel built of red cedar, and a remarkable fast sailer; also her Cargo, consisting of melasses and sugar:*
>   *The Sloop* NANCY, *and Cargo of tar, pitch, turpentine and rice.*
>   *And on Saturday the 11th inst. At Col. Nicholas Stilwill's, will be sold,*
>   *The Schooner* HENRY, *likewise her Cargo, consisting of 20 hhds.* [hogsheads] *of sugar, 15 hhds. Of melasses. 7 hhds. Of rum, a quantity of cotton and coffee.*
>   *By order of the Court of Admiralty,* JOSEPH POTTS, *Marshall*

New-Jersey, September 4, 1779.
On Saturday the 18th instant, at eight o'clock, at the house of John Brick, Esq. on Morris's River, WILL begin the Sales of the CARGO of the Brig captured by Captain Stilwill, in the schooner Hawke, consisting of 200 puncheons of old Jamaica spirits, and a quantity of old Madeira wines.

At the same time will be sold said BRIG, with her appurtenances, per inventory.

By Order of the Court of Admiralty,
2w JOSEPH POTTS, Marshal.

This advertisement refers to the prize brig *Lyon*, captured by Enoch Stillwell. Note that the auction site is well up the Maurice River out of the reach of British vessels, *New-Jersey Gazette*, September 8, 1779. *Courtesy of the American Antiquarian Society.*

The receipt book of Colonel Richard Somers covering the years 1774–83 reveals what may be the most comprehensive breakdown of the liquidation and the payout of a prize to the various investors, captain and crew of a privateer vessel in the mid-Atlantic region during the Revolution. In particular, one page in Colonel Somers's receipt book lists investors and/or vendors of the privateer schooner *Hawk* as follows:

1779
Nov 11ᵗʰ Acct. of Bills and Orders Excepted & Moneys Rcd. Of Mr Joseph Potts, Marshall on Act. of the Prize Schooner Henry *and the Brig* Lyon *Capt. [captured] by the Schooner* Hawk

Doct. Rennards	*Order*	*£5192 14=6*
Thomas Leaming	*Bill*	*3655*
John Murre	*Ditto*	*19242 = 3*
Christopher Rape	*Do* [Ditto]	*7557 = 17*
Capt. E Stillwell	*Do*	*3125 = 12*
Thomas Sinnickson	*Do*	*19542 = 17*
Richd Somers	*Do*	*578*
Robart Snell	*Do*	*3255 = 8*
Jesse Hand	*Do*	*3230 = 16*
Mount Skeen [Mounce Keen]	*Do*	*1479 =*
Robart Matlocks	*Do*	*1776*
Jacob Robarts	*Do*	*1710 = 10*
Henry Winecoop	*Order*	*2712 = 16*
		£73058 = 13 6

1779

November 11th — Acct of Bills and
Orders Exicepted & Moneys Recd of
Mr. Joseph Potts, Marshall on Acct
of the Prize Schooner Henry & the Brig
Lyon Capd by the Schooner Hawk

Doct. Quennards Order	£	5192 = 14 = 6
Thomas Lerming Bill		3655
John Murre — Ditto		19242 = 3
Christopher Nape Do		7557 = 17
Capt E. Stillwell Do		3125 = 12
Thomas Simmkson Do		19542 = 17
Richd Somers — Do		578
Robart Snell — Do		3255 = 8
Jesse Hand — Do		3230 = 16
Mount Skeen — Do		1479 =
Robart Mattocks Do		1776 =
Jacob Robarts — Do		1710 = 10
Henry Wincoop Order		2712 = 16
	£	73058 = 13 6

Investors in the privateer schooner *Hawk* from Richard Somers's receipt book. *Private collection.*

While no roster of the fifty-man crew of the privateer *Hawk* has been found to date, Richard Somers's receipt book records large payments made to what could be described as a who's-who of Cape May privateer captains. The individual entries are vague as to whether the payees were investors or members of Captain Stillwell's crew, but most of those listed are known owners of the *Hawk* (see chapter 4). Some of the captains listed below, such as Treen, Griffing and James Willets, may have served as officers under Enoch Stillwell on a vessel of this size.

Payments made by Richard Somers for "Prize money in the Schooner Henry *& the Brig* Lyon*" include:*

Enoch Stillwell	*£20729 = 5*
Enoch Stillwell	*£5000*
William Treen	*£4000*
John Holmes	*£4500*
Sarah Griffing [for Moses Griffing]	*£5000*
John Bray [sold by Robert Snell]	*£5418 = 15 − 3*
James Willets	*£22219 = 11 − 1*
J Goldin	*£4366 = 7 − 6*
Christopher Rape	*£10,000*

You might say Enoch Stillwell was destined to be a privateer captain. He was a direct descendant of John Stillwell and Thomas Hand, who were among the earliest whalers to settle at Cape May. His parents, Captain Nicholas Stillwell Sr. and Sarah Hand Stillwell, were both raised on or near Cape Island and lived there until Nicholas Sr. purchased a plantation at the opposite end of the county overlooking the Great Egg Harbor Bay. Throughout his childhood, Enoch would have seen merchant vessels (including those captained by his father) sailing in and out of the Bay. From the second-floor windows of the family's plantation house, he could have looked across the bay, over Peck's Beach and out to the open sea to watch for sails approaching the Cape.

As an adult, Enoch served as a master of locally owned merchant vessels before and after the Revolution. He and his elder brother Colonel Nicholas Stillwell were both "field officers" in the Cape May Militia during the war. Enoch's younger brother David Stillwell served as a privateer crewman, and two of his sisters were married to Cape May privateer captains. His brother-in-law Colonel Richard Somers served as the banker for the county's privateers and owned privateer vessels with the Stillwells and other local

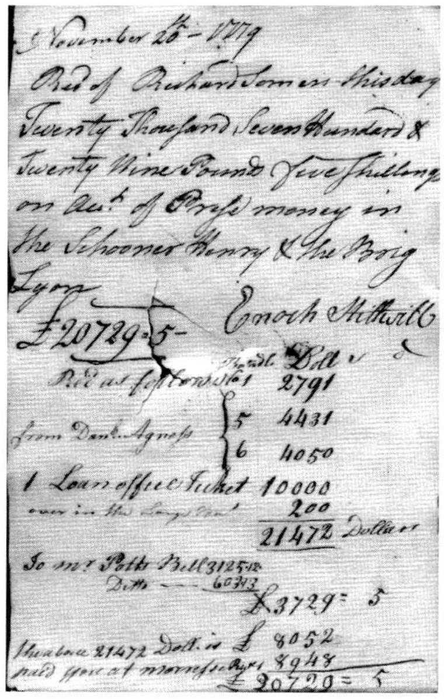

Payment to Captain Enoch Stillwell "on acct. of Prize money in the Schooner Henry & the Brig Lyon," from Richard Somers's receipt book. *Private collection.*

investors. Enoch's father's cousin Captain John Stillwell was one of the best-known mariners on the East Coast and was himself a privateer during the war.

On December 6, 1780, letters of marque were issued for the Pennsylvania ship *Morning Star*, with Enoch serving as mate (second in command) under Jeremiah Simmons, master. This vessel had twice the crew of the *Hawk*, one hundred, and almost double the firepower at eighteen guns and was owned by Francis Gurney & Co. Gurney was a merchant and Pennsylvania militia colonel with business ties to the Cape May privateers, so it is likely that his fellow investors in the *Morning Star* were many of the same Cape May men who had invested in the *Hawk*.

The letters of marque for the *Morning Star* also record a physical description of the privateer: "Enoch Stillwell, Lieutenant. Of the age of thirty five years. Stature five feet eight inches, dark hair & dark complexion." Enoch was commissioned a first major in the Cape May Militia on September 20, 1776, at the age of thirty-one and promoted to lieutenant colonel on March 27, 1778. According to British war records, Enoch Stillwell was imprisoned on the notorious prison ship *Jersey*. At some point after Stillwell took the *Lyon* and *Henry*, the British and Tories captured the *Hawk*. On March 3, 1834, about fifty years after the fact, Jacob Garretson stated in his Revolutionary War pension application that

> *he next volunteered under Capt Enoch Stillwell and went on board of the Schooner* Hawk, *and was taken a prisoner by the tories & refugees _____ _____ & then into New York & put on a prisonship called The* Guard House *& kept on board of said ship one month & was then exchanged & returned home.…Then volunteered under Capt Simmonds & went on board of a twenty gun ship called the* Morning Star, *and was taken by the* Medea *Frigate, & by the British taken to Charleston South Carolina,*

& then put on board of a prison ship & kept a prisoner nine months—then made my escape with two others John McDonald & William _______ & returned to Gloucester in the fall of 1781.

First as captain of the *Hawk* and second as the mate of the privateer ship *Morning Star*, Stillwell appears to have been captured twice during the course of the war. Word of the capture of that vessel came out of British-occupied New York as reported in the *New York Gazette* of February 19, 1781:

NEW-YORK, February 19.
His Majesty's Ship the Medea, *Capt Duncan, that sailed from hence some Time ago for South Carolina, on her Passage took the following Vessels— The Ship* Morning-Star, *a Rebel Privateer belonging to Philadelphia, of 18 Guns, and 100 Men, commanded by Jeremiah Symonds* [Simmons]. *The Schooner* Blossom *laden with Tobacco, bound from this Continent to St. Eustatia. A Brig and a Sloop, whose Names we have not learnt. The* Morning-Star *and* Blossom, *had arrived,* [at New York] *but the Brig and Sloop were missing.*

As for the personal life of Enoch Stillwell, on August 28, 1768, he married Sarah Savage, the daughter of Joseph and Martha Daniels Savage of Cape May County. Enoch and Sarah were the parents of Martha, Savage, Sarah, Anna and Sophia Stillwell. Enoch lost his wife toward the end of the Revolution on March 19, 1782, and he died about five years later, on January 31, 1787. It appears that Enoch Stillwell remarried after his first wife's death though no marriage record has been found to date. A surviving letter was apparently written by a second wife, Phebe Stillwell, to Enoch's brother-in-law Colonel Richard Somers. The letter was written on the day Enoch Stillwell died and gives a clear picture of his last day on earth and his dying wishes:

Dr Sir   Cape May Janry 31ˢᵗ 1787
I am truly sorry this should inform you of the heavy loss we have met with, in losing an affectionate Husband, a loving Brother, and a tender Parent He departed this life (this morning about half after seven oclock) and his dying request was and hoped in God that you woud prove and affectionate Guardian to his helpless offspring, and look into his affairs, and settle them if possible, he died without a Will, and was at times very delirious, but was so that he knew he was advancing to the Verge of Eternity, and the

only thing that seemed to trouble him was his Children he met his fate with that seeming fortitude as became a Christian but still had a desire to live, My Mind is in such a state that I hardly know what I am about, if any blemishes shoud appear in this short, but truly affecting Epithe, [epitaph] hope you will excuse, take the matter home to yourself and Judge of my unfortunate situation in leaving so tender a companion

I beg you will inform Sister Griffin [Sarah Stillwell Griffing, wife of Captain Moses Griffing] *of this and pray let me hear from you by the bearer Mr Benj Orum*
I am D [Dear] *Sir Your Affecty* [Affectionately]
Phebe Stillwill

Surprisingly, Enoch Stillwell, like many of the movers and shakers involved in the Cape May privateer trade, died intestate. Enoch's second wife, Phebe, and Eli Eldredge were appointed administrators of the estate. Like many of his peers, Enoch Stillwell died not long after the end of the Revolution, but unlike many of those peers, he seems to have fared well financially through the conflict and the currency depreciation, market instability and so forth that was the result of the upheaval of society during that time. His inventory, which reflects movable property only, not his extensive land holdings, was appraised by his distant cousin Jesse Hand along with Thomas Shaw:

An Inventory of the Goods, Chattels, Rights, and Credits of Colonel Enoch Stillwill of the County of Cape May Late Deceased, Apraised by Jesse Hand and Thomas Shaw, July 3d, 1787.

Viz / To Cash and Clothing	*£41 "4 "5*
Bonds, Bills and Book Debts	*1496 "14 "9*
Shop Goods	*43 "19 "0*
Negroes	*115 "0 "0*
Household Goods, Beds etc	*89 "14 "6*
Cattle, Horses, Sheep and Swine	*277 "0 "9*
Meat and Grain	*65 "5 "0*
Loan Office Certificates	*167 "2 "11*
Plantation & Farming Tools	*90 "3 "6*
	2386 "4 "8
Bad Debts	*106 "5 "2*
Total	*2552 "9 "10*

Taken and Apraised by us Jesse Hand
Thomas Shaw   *The Day and Year Above*

As can be seen by the inventory, Enoch Stillwell was typical of the men of the elite families of colonial Cape May; though he was a ship captain by profession and apparently owned a store, like his whaler-yeomen father and grandfather, he was first and foremost a farmer.

As for Enoch Stillwell's "helpless offspring," they were well cared for by their loving and extremely wealthy uncle. Lieutenant Colonel Enoch Stillwell's final wishes were fulfilled as his brother-in-law Colonel Richard Somers, now of Philadelphia, was appointed guardian of three of the youngest children, Savage, Sophia and Anna. Like many families of Cape May's merchant class, the children appear to have alternately lived in Philadelphia and Cape May or Great Egg Harbour Township, Gloucester County.

The eldest child, Martha Stillwell, was not quite of age (seventeen) when her father died but doesn't appear to have chosen a guardian, as did three of her younger siblings. She married Joseph Hildreth of Cape May County two years after her father's death and died two years after her marriage in 1791, likely during childbirth. On April 1, 1793, two years after becoming a widower, Joseph Hildreth married Anna, his deceased wife's second-youngest sister. If the existing birth and marriage records are correct, Anna was only fifteen years of age when she married Joseph Hildreth and became the stepmother of her sister's daughter, Lydia Hildreth. She would bear the first of her own five children at age seventeen.

Enoch Stillwell's second-eldest daughter, Sarah, who was about eleven years of age when her father died, doesn't appear to have chosen a guardian, and no marriage record has been found for her. Sophia, the youngest child, was unmarried and living in Cape May County in 1799, and no marriage record has been found to date

Enoch's only son, Savage Stillwell, became a mariner like his father and grandfather. In time, he would go on to become a prominent Philadelphia merchant and ship owner in partnership with Captain William Jonas Keen, who was a descendant of one of the earliest Swedish families to settle along the Delaware. (Another of that clan, Captain Nicholas Keen of the Salem County militia, shared command of New Jersey state gunboats with privateer Colonel Elijah Hand during the Revolution.)

The story of Savage Stillwell and his business partner is a classic example of how the political, business and marital connections tied merchant families together before, during and after the Revolution. Savage Stillwell would marry Susannah Mason in 1800. She was the daughter of British-born Philadelphia ship captain Thomas Mason. In 1793, William Jonas Keen married Sarah Somers, who was Savage's first cousin and the daughter of his legal guardian, Colonel Richard Somers. Captain Keen's cousin Sarah Keen Austin became the second wife of Commodore John Barry, and his sister Elizabeth Keen married Commodore Barry's nephew Captain Patrick Hayes.

Approximately twelve years after the death of Enoch Stillwell, Benjamin Franklin's grandnephew, attorney Franklin Davenport of Woodbury, New Jersey, wrote a letter to William Jonas Keen that sheds light on the financial circumstances involving a Revolution-era guardian/ward relationship:

D. Sr. Whilst I was in Cape May last month, a Miss Sophia Stillwell, asked my directions about Settling what little monies were coming to her from the estate of Richard Somers Esq [?] her late Guardian & Uncle—in order to Ascertain how much Money was received by the Guardian, I had to examine the Office at Cape May I procured Some Information from Mr Giles [?]—The Result is—

1. A Judgment obtained by Col. Somers against Benj Laurence for £200 - 0 - 0 with Int. [interest] 20 April 1788

2. A Judgment against John Cathcart for 84—with Int. 15 June 1790

3. a Judgment agst. The Estate of Joseph Savage her Grandfather for 727 – 6 – 2¾ with Int. 27. Oct. 1790

By the above you will observe, better than £1000 have come to the Col's Hands for the use of Anna & Sophia Stillwell—I wish to know if there are any payments to or receipts by either of the Girls or Mr Hildreth who married Anna—when I had the papers of Col. Somers I recollect seeing something concerning the above—I wait your answer to give Information to the Girls—with Compliments to Mrs. Keen [Colonel Richard Somers's daughter]

I am with esteem

Yours   F. Davenport

Capt Keen Woodbury N J Aug. 1799

In addition to practicing law in Gloucester County, New Jersey, Franklin Davenport Esq. was a veteran of the Revolution, enlisting as a private and later attaining the rank of major general in the New Jersey Militia. He also served as a senator and representative from his home state. Davenport, like fellow attorney and future governor Joseph Bloomfield, provided legal counsel to many of the privateer families of South Jersey. While most sources vaguely refer to Davenport as the nephew of Benjamin Franklin, research suggests the he was a grandnephew, the son of nephew

Josiah Franklin Davenport (who was the son of Benjamin Franklin's sister, Sarah Franklin Davenport).

An interesting footnote to the story of the capture of the *Henry* and the *Lyon* concerns a lawsuit for large cash damages against Captain Enoch Stillwell that was filed by Delaware Bay pilot Matthew Hand in the New Jersey Supreme Court. Both men were direct descendants of Thomas Hand, the whaler, and were, in fact, second cousins. (Matthew Hand is the third great-grandfather of one author of this book, DPS.) Matthew distinguished himself as a pilot probably before and definitely after the Revolution. In June 1779, Matthew had been engaged by Stillwell to serve as second mate aboard the privateer schooner *Hawk*. Hand was offered three shares of any prizes taken from the British as compensation for his service for a period of six months. The *Lyon* and *Henry* were captured in the first week of September 1779, with both vessels subsequently sold at public auction. For reasons unknown, Captain Stillwell allegedly refused to pay Hand his fair share of the prizes, which amounted to the significant sum of £3,000. Perhaps Matthew Hand wasn't aboard the *Hawk* when the prizes were taken? Hand claimed fraud and took the case to the New Jersey Supreme Court. His lawyer was the very famous attorney and future governor of New Jersey Joseph Bloomfield. Bloomfield had been a major in the New Jersey militia and later a judge. He was also the registrar of the Court of the Admiralty for the province of New Jersey before the Revolution and was very familiar with admiralty law. Later he was appointed brigadier general in the U.S. Army and served in Congress from 1817 to 1821. Enoch Stillwell hired no less a prominent attorney than Elias Boudinot, the erstwhile president of the Continental Congress. Stillwell's defense stated that Hand's claim against him had no force in law and was not duly sworn by the defendant. This was indeed a pretty shaky defense, as all officers and crew were granted a specific share of prizes captured by privateers. Although there is no definitive statement as to the outcome, it appears from a copy of the case that Matthew Hand was awarded more than £3,000 to cover his claim and probably court costs.

12

PRIVATEERS, TAVERNS AND RUM

J.P. HAND

IT IS SAFE TO SAY that many of Cape May's privateers had more assets after the Revolution than they had before the conflict began. This was especially true among the owners and captains, as shown in surviving estate inventories, wills and land deeds. These various documents list cash on hand, debts due, value of movable property (including vessels, mills and slaves), as well as real estate owned.

The Cape May County Quarterly Court records illustrate another way in which many of the major players of the Cape May privateer trade prospered during and shortly after the Revolution. In addition to the usual lawsuits and indictments for minor offenses, the court books list the petitions and approvals for tavern licenses. The records show that a majority of the applicants during that time were connected to the privateer trade in one way or another. Six of the eight applicants listed below were Cape May privateer captains, while almost half were merchants as well. Note that many of the "sureties" (guarantors) of these tavern keepers were privateers and, in many cases, were tavern keepers themselves:

> *Moses Griffin[g] Licensed to keep Publick House in the upper precinct where he now Dwelleth for one year Ensuing—Moses Griffin and his Sureties John Cathcart and Israel Stites—Bound in Recognizance According to the Statute in the Sum of Twenty Pounds for his keeping good order as Inn or Tavern Keeper*

May Sessions and Term 1784

Captain James Willits Presents Petition for License to keep a Publick House or Inn of Entertainment at the House wherein he now Dwells in the upper Precinct of the County of Cape May; which is Granted the said James Willits is Bound to the State in the Sum of £20. And Enoch Stillwell and Henry Young his Sureties in £20 each [one of Willits's surities, Henry Young was indicted for assault and battery at the previous court session, February 1784].

February Sessions and Term 1784
Daniel Hand Presents Petition for License to keep a Publick House or Inn of Entertainment at the House where he now Dwells in the Middle Precinct of the County of Cape May, which is Granted, the said Daniel Hand bound to the State in the Sum of £20—and Nicholas Stillwill and Phillip Hand Sureties in £20 eac

George Taylor, Presents a Petition to keep a Publick House, or Inn of Entertainment, at the House wherein he now Dwells in the Lower Precinct of the said County which is Granted the said George Tay[lor] *is Bound to the State in the Sum of £20—and Memucan Hughes and Ellis Hughes Jr. his Sureties, in the Sum of £20 each*

Others among the privateers of Cape May who established taverns during or just after the war or continued to operate their existing ones included:

- Colonel Nicholas Stillwell (investor/captain) with sureties, John Stites (privateer officer) and Joshua Garretson
- Israel Stites, (privateer captain and investor), Upper Precinct
- Daniel Hand, (privateer captain), Lower Precinct, sureties Jedediah Hughes and Abraham Woolson
- Abraham Bennet (privateer captain), Lower Precinct

Taverns were few in number in colonial Cape May County and were closely regulated as to the behavior that took place in them, hence the need for sureties. The "Tavern or Inn of Entertainment" was almost always operated out of the licensee's home. The process of regulation and licensing differed little from that used back in the early towns of Long Island, New York, where the grandparents or great-grandparents of many of these men had lived.

A citizen of good standing with the capital needed to operate a tavern (and extend credit to his patrons) applied for a license with other upright citizens as sureties. The tavern keeper would continue to be licensed for as long as he kept order at his establishment. Interestingly, many of the county's taverns also served as general stores, and at least one employed a schoolmaster to educate "scholars."

It should come as no surprise that a high number of the Revolutionary War–era tavern keepers in the county were privateers. Hundreds of years of literature and popular culture would suggest that mariners and taverns go together like bread and butter. What could possibly warm the heart of a mariner and veteran of the Revolution more than presiding over his own tavern, drinking his own rum and telling the tales of his exploits during the war?

We can visualize the typical eighteenth-century privateer captain of Cape May; he owned a plantation of a few hundred acres, where with his wife and daughters and sons, he raised free-range cattle and grew corn, wheat and rye for sustenance and income. If he (or his father) was particularly well heeled, he also owned investment properties in the form of valuable cedar swamps and upland timber, which were harvested for export products in various forms. Like his yeoman ancestors on Long Island, in

State of New-Jersey, March 20th, 1780.

TO BE SOLD,

AT public vendue, on the 30th inst. at the house of Col. Richard Somers, at Great-Egg-Harbour, in the county of Gloucester, precisely at ten o'clock in the forenoon, the Prize SLOOP Hazard, lately captured by Capt. Wm. Treen, as she now lies at said place; together with her Sails, Tackle, &c. also her CARGO, consisting of Rum, Sugar, Molasses, Coffee, &c. &c.

By order of the Judge of the Court of Admiralty,

ZACH. ROSSELL, Marshal.

N. B. The Marshal requests those who intend purchasing at said sales, that they furnish themselves with the cash, as no credit will be given.

The sale of the prize sloop *Hazard*, captured by Cape May's Captain William Treen, *New-Jersey Gazette*, March 22, 1780. *Courtesy of the American Antiquarian Society.*

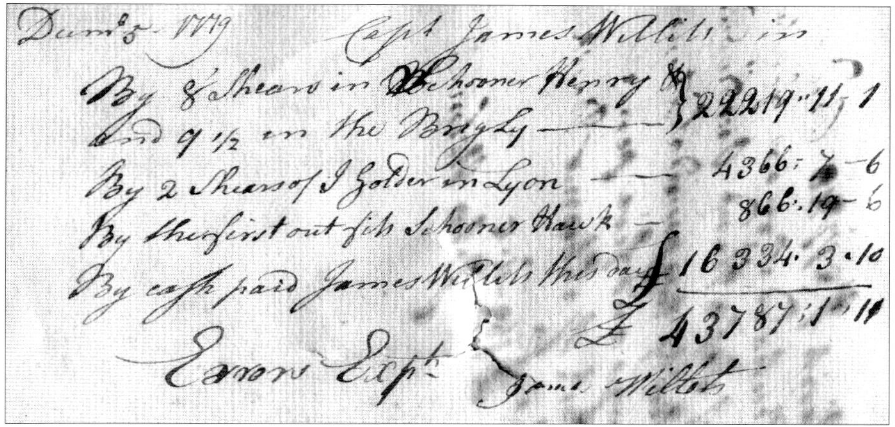

Payments to Captain James Willets for privateer *Hawk* and prizes, *Lyon* and *Henry*, from Richard Somers's receipt book. *Private collection.*

New England or back in Old England, he was concerned with increasing his wealth through hard work and shrewd business dealings. Owning a tavern was icing on the cake, so to speak, where the cash rolled in as long as you minded to whom credit was given.

Not only were taverns regulated in regard to licensing and conduct, but also the prices allowed for services and refreshments were predetermined on an almost yearly basis by the Cape May County Courts. The court records of tavern fees transcribed below, two from the middle of the war, one from two decades after, give a clear picture of what might have been provided in the way of entertainment:

February Term	*1778*
Tavern Fees	
To a Breakfast or Supper of Coffee or Tea	*£0 – 5 – 0*
To a Do [Ditto] of Country Produce	*2 – –*
To a Dinner of Do	*– 6*
To a Dinner Extraordinary	*3 – 6*
To a Gill of Whiskey	*1 – 0*
To a Gill of Peach Brandy	*1 – 3*
To a Mugg of Metheglin [honey mead]	*4 – 0*
To a Mugg of Cider	*1 – 0*
To a Nights Lodging	*0 – 6*
To a Nights Pasturing a Horse	*1 – 3*

To a Night Stabling a Horse with Salt Hay   *1 - 6*
To 2 Quarts of Oats or Indian Corn   *1 – 0*

This Regulation to take effect the first Day of March
Next Ensuing

27ᵗʰ Day of May 1778
Tavern Rates & Fees
To a Gill of West Indies Rum   *£ - 1 - - 6*
To a Bowl of Mim with ½ [Rum?]   *4 - - -*
To a Do of Grog   *3 - - -*
To a Gill of Whiskey   *--- - 9*
To a Gill of Ginn or Brandy   *1 - - 3*
All Destilled Liquers not named   *1 - - 3*
To a Quart of Cider   *1 - - -*
To a Quart of Strong Beer   *1 - - 3*
To a Quart of Metheglin or Cyder Royal   *2 - - 6*
To a Bowl of Fruit Punch   *5 - - 6*
To a Do of Milk Punch   *4 - - -*
To a Do of Egg Punch   *5 - - -*
To a Breakfast   *1 - - 6*
To a Dinner   *1 - - 9*
To a Supper   *1 - - 6*
To a Nights Lodging   *- - - 6*
To 2 Quarts of Oats or Indian Corn   *- - - 7*
To a pasturing a Horse a Night   *- - 10*
To a Nights Stableing a Horse Salt Hay   *- - 10*
To a Nights Stableing a Horse Clover Hay   *1 - - 9*

Ordinance of Tavern Rates
May Session 1806

Breakfast   *$ 0 – 25 cents*
Dinner   *36 ½*
Supper   *25*
Nights Lodging for one Person in a Bed   *12½*
Do [ditto] *for 2 each*   *9*
One [gill] *of West India Rum*   *10*
Nip of Mint or Toddy   *12½*

Bowel of Toddy	*25*
Bowel of Punch	*37½*
Bowel of Egg Punch	*33½*
Sling or Do	*16*
Pint of Madaria wine	*50*
Pint of Lisbon wine	*37½*
Pint of Sherry Do	*37½*
Pint of Teneriff [Canary Island]	*25*
Bowel of sangria	*25*
Bowel of Brandy Toddy	*25*
Mug of Strong Beer	*12½*
Mug of Cider	*10*
One Quart of Oats or Indian Corn	*4*
One Night Stabling a Horse with fres[h] *hay*	*25*
Do of salt hay	*12*
Do for every 24 hours	*12½*

As can be seen by the tavern rates, a large variety of spirits, wine and mixed drinks were offered at public houses in the "backwater" county of Cape May. That fact, while surprising, is easily explainable. Cape May was the least populated county in New Jersey both before and after the American Revolution. Since its inception in 1692, locally owned vessels had been making trading voyages to the Caribbean to the south and New England to the north. By the time of the Revolution, Cape May captains had long been traversing the Atlantic to trade in European ports and venturing south to ports in Central and South America as well.

The Coffee House in Philadelphia was the site of many of the public auctions of privateer vessels during the Revolution, *Pennsylvania Packet,* April 18, 1782. *Courtesy of the American Antiquarian Society.*

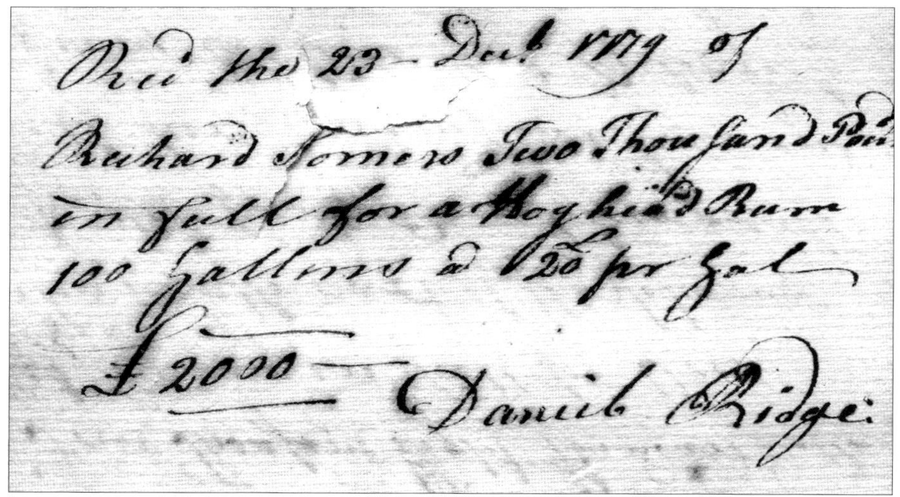

A receipt for a hogshead of rum from the *Lyon*, from Richard Somers's receipt book. *Private collection*.

During the war years, it is likely that much of the rum and imported European wines served in the county's taverns came from British merchant ships taken as prizes by local privateers. In fact, the ledgers of Thomas Leaming Jr. and Colonel Richard Somers record instances of local privateers and investors receiving large quantities of alcoholic beverages in lieu of cash payment. Interestingly, the tavern rates show that in colonial Cape May, the cost of a night's stabling for a horse was two to four times that of a night's lodging for a man.

EPILOGUE

J.P. HAND

Just how much of an impact could the men and vessels of the Cape May Navy possibly have had against the might of the world's greatest naval force? After all, the privateers of Cape May could at best do little more than harass only the smallest vessels of the British navy. And though the county's privateers took a substantial number of prizes during the war, in the grand scheme of things, that effort only represented a relatively minor financial burden to the British merchant fleet.

Perhaps the effects of the efforts of the Cape May privateers and privateers in general could be compared to a dull toothache endured by an eighteenth-century British soldier, not life-threatening but more of a constant source of annoyance. Or perhaps their endeavors were comparable to an arsonist setting fires at multiple locations over a period of years. Military historians can argue the minute details of the Revolution and the various factors that led to the American victory. The fact is, the story of the privateers of Cape May is a small part in the fight for Independence—but a story that deserves to be told in detail. In one place and one time, in a window of seven years, a relatively small group of men from one community, many related by blood, came together and fought for a cause they believed in. These privateers, most of whom had no military experience before the war, had a lot to gain and a lot to lose.

Because the English colonies in America were successful in their fight for independence, these men of Cape May, like their counterparts throughout the colonies, were then and are to this day considered Patriots. Had the forces of Great Britain been able to put down the rebellion, these same men would have continued to be viewed as traitors to their King and would have been at the mercy of the British government and the Loyalists who had fought so fiercely against them. They would have lost their lands and other assets, if not their freedom or their lives.

As it was, the satisfaction and thankfulness felt by the captains, owners and investors of the Cape May Navy were in many cases short-lived. In Cape May and the adjoining counties, the leaders of the rebellion, the political leaders and militia officers, tended to be men of middle age with assets and stature in their communities. With much shorter average lifespans in the eighteenth century and medical practices that seem barbaric by today's standards, it should come as no surprise that many of those leaders would die in their fifties or sixties.

Most of the hostilities between the fledgling United States of America and Great Britain ended in 1783, and within a few decades, many of the movers and shakers involved in the privateer trade at Cape May passed away. Like the great Patriot Benjamin Franklin (1706–1790), most of the important figures of the Cape's privateer trade died in the last decade of the eighteenth century:

Colonel Elijah Hand	d. 1790
Jesse Hand Esq.	d. 1791
Jonathan Hand Esq.	d. 1790
John Holmes Sr.	d. 1790
Aaron Leaming Jr.	d. 1780
Thomas Leaming Esq.	d. 1797
Colonel Richard Somers	d. 1795
Lieutenant Colonel Enoch Stillwell	d. 1787
Colonel Nicholas Stillwell	d. 1792

It should be noted that while some of Cape May's privateer captains fit the profile described above, the majority of them were in their early to mid-twenties during their privateering days.

Captains John Stillwell and William Treen received letters of marque at the age of thirty-seven and twenty-nine, respectively, while Enoch Stillwell captained the privateer schooner *Hawk* at age thirty-four. The old man in the group was Colonel Elijah Hand, who commanded the state boat of New Jersey, *Enterprize*, in 1782 at the age of fifty-two.

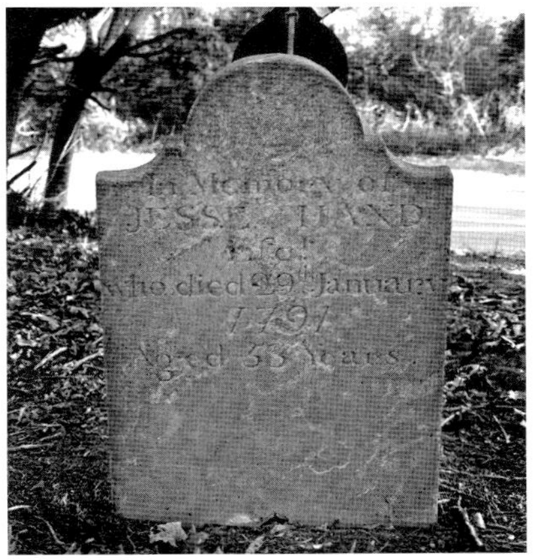 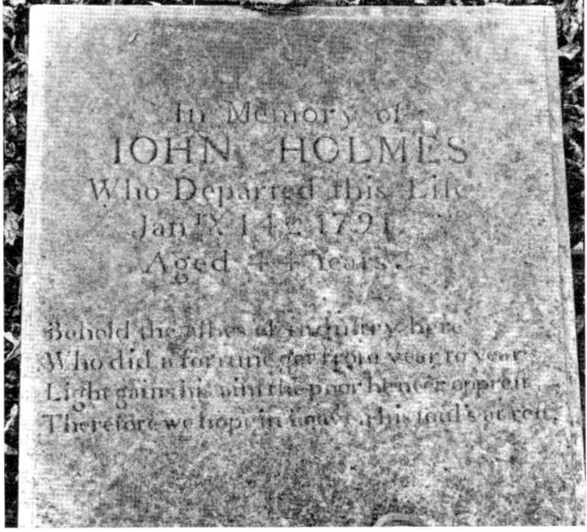

Left: The headstone of Jesse Hand Esq. (Hand family burial ground), Swainton, New Jersey. *Right*: John Holmes Sr. (Holmes family burial ground), Cape May Court House, New Jersey. *Photos by Jim Talone*.

The old saying "It's an old man's war, but a young man's fight" comes to mind when examining the letters of marque issued to many of the Cape May privateers. It is remarkable that young men barely out of their teens could shoulder the responsibility of commanding an armed vessel during wartime, when at sea their word was the final say. They not only risked their own lives but the lives of their crewmen as well. In addition, the privateer captains were responsible for the financial investment incurred by the vessel's owners and had to abide by the terms of the letters of marque issued to them in regard to what prizes they could legally take and how those prizes could be disposed of. Letters of marque records reveal the tender age at which many of the Cape May privateers served as captains and mates:

John Badcock	25
Joseph Badcock	23
Joseph Edwards	21
Silas Foster	24
Isaac Swain	25
James Swain	23
Uriah Swain	23
William Treen	29
Enoch Willet	25
Hope Willet	24

Sadly, some of the young privateer captains died during or shortly after the war. As previously mentioned, Captain Humphrey Hughes and his twenty-five-man crew in the *New Comet* were lost at sea in or about 1778 (allegedly run down by a British warship). Captain Hope Willets died the year after the war ended in 1784, leaving one daughter, Hopewell Willets. On January 22, 1781, William Treen in the privateer brig *Fame* barely escaped death when his vessel overturned in a gale, "while lying off Egg Harbour." Captain Treen and a few of his crewmen survived, while it was reported that twenty-five of his crew drowned. The *Fame* had only two weeks earlier captured the Loyalist privateer schooner *Cock*, which was on a cruise from New York to the Chesapeake Bay in search of American prizes.

With the signing of the Treaty of Paris on September 3, 1783, the war between Great Britain and the United States officially came to an end. While no land battles or skirmishes were fought on Cape May County soil, a heavy price was paid by the populace, especially among the privateer captains and crew. For the families of Humphrey Hughes and his crew and those of the crewmen aboard William Treen's *Fame*, life would never be the same. In addition to those privateers who lost their lives in the struggle for independence, dozens more Cape May men endured cruel and sometimes fatal treatment at the hands of the British while confined in the notorious prison ships of New York.

The most infamous of these was the prison hulk *Jersey*, in which an estimated eight thousand American soldiers and mariners were held over the course of the war. Men of Cape May who were held in the ship nicknamed *Hell* included privateer captains and officers Elijah Hand (*Enterprize*, twenty-five men), Moses Griffing (brig *Argo*, seventy-five men), Enoch Stillwell (schooner *Hawk*, fifty men), John Stillwell, Israel Stites,

PHILADELPHIA.

From the beſt authority we learn that the ſtate of Maryland hath agreed to the confederation of the United States, by which means the confederacy is now compleat.

We alſo learn that the ſtate of Virginia have given up their claim to the back lands, and have, in a formal manner, by a law, ceded to the United States all the lands lying to the weſtward of the River Ohio.

The brig Fame, Capt. Treen, about fourteen days ago, took the privateer ſchooner Cock, Capt. Brooks, bound from New-York on a cruize to Cheſapeak Bay, and ſent her into a port in New-Jerſey.

We hear the brig Fame, Capt. Treen, lying in Egg-Harbour, in the gale of wind on the 22d inſtant, was overſet, and it is ſaid twenty-five of her hands were drowned.

Report of the capture of the Tory privateer schooner *Cock* by Captain William Treen in the brig *Fame* and the subsequent capsizing of the *Fame* within days, with a loss of twenty-five crew members, *Pennsylvania Journal*, April 27, 1780. *Courtesy of the American Antiquarian Society.*

William Treen and James Willets. It can be assumed that the vessels and crew commanded by those captains were captured at the same time. The number of crewmen on board each privateer was dependent on the size of the vessel and number of guns (cannons).

The brutal treatment received by Patriots taken by British and Loyalist forces seems to have been in sharp contrast to that shown to those taken prisoner by American forces, whether on land or at sea. For example, a Captain Childs was the master of the British brig *Lyon* when it fell to Cape May's Captain Enoch Stillwell and the *Hawk* in 1779. Apparently, Captain Childs was either injured in the altercation or fell ill afterward. An entry in the receipt book of Colonel Richard Somers shows payment made to John Holmes, "for the use of John Creysey & wife eighty two pounds for Bording Nursing & Doctoring Capt Childs Prisoner."

While the treatment shown many American prisoners during the Revolution was horrific and would be considered war crimes by today's standards, it can be understood, if not justified by a number of factors. The British forces seemed to look upon the "rebels" with the contempt due to traitors to their mother country, while the Loyalists shared that scorn but also experienced the added desperation of having lost everything they had in their native (or adopted) land.

After the war, life in Cape May County returned to a more normal pace. By far the most mysterious character involved in the Cape May privateer trade was Captain Yelverton Taylor. His service as a Delaware Bay pilot and privateer captain just prior to and during the Revolution was reported in contemporary news accounts, though many of the details of his life remain unknown at this time. A baptismal record from the First Presbyterian Church of Philadelphia dated October 1, 1753, lists a Yelverton Taylor as the child of Elias and Mary Taylor.

Captain Yelverton Taylor may have been born in Philadelphia, but if that is the case, then it is very likely that his parents were from Cape May. Many clues suggest a Cape May connection, but just the fact that he was a Delaware Bay pilot alone would indicate ties to Cape May or Lewes, Delaware. In addition, the privateer vessels he captained were owned by Cape May investors, and many of his crewman were from Cape May, including likely relatives Matthias Taylor, John Snider (alias John Taylor) and John McCormick (married to Mary Taylor of Cape May).

His given name is another clue; the authors believe he was named for early Cape May settler Yelverton Crowell. Furthermore, after the Revolution (1784), prominent Cape May merchant George Taylor named a son Yelverton, obviously in honor of the privateer captain. While reporting on Captain Taylor's privateering exploits, at least one Philadelphia paper refers to the captain as "of Egg Harbour," the common name used for the area surrounding the Great Egg Harbor Bay separating Cape May and Atlantic Counties.

The greatest mystery of all concerning Taylor is what became of the celebrated privateer after the war. The last available record for the captain appears in a Philadelphia tax list for the year 1780 (one year after the last news account of his wartime activities). The entry shows a payment made "for Yelverton Taylor" for property located in the city's Dock Ward. Others connected to our story who paid taxes in that neighborhood in that year were Captain (John) Stillwell, Thomas Leaming Jr., Francis Gurney and Stephen Decatur Sr.

After many years of searching through private and public records, the authors have found no trace of the whereabouts of Yelverton Taylor in postwar America—no will, death record, marriage record, pension application or deed. He may have been lost at sea, died in a British prison or headed west after the war. Hopefully an answer will surface someday as to what became of this true American hero.

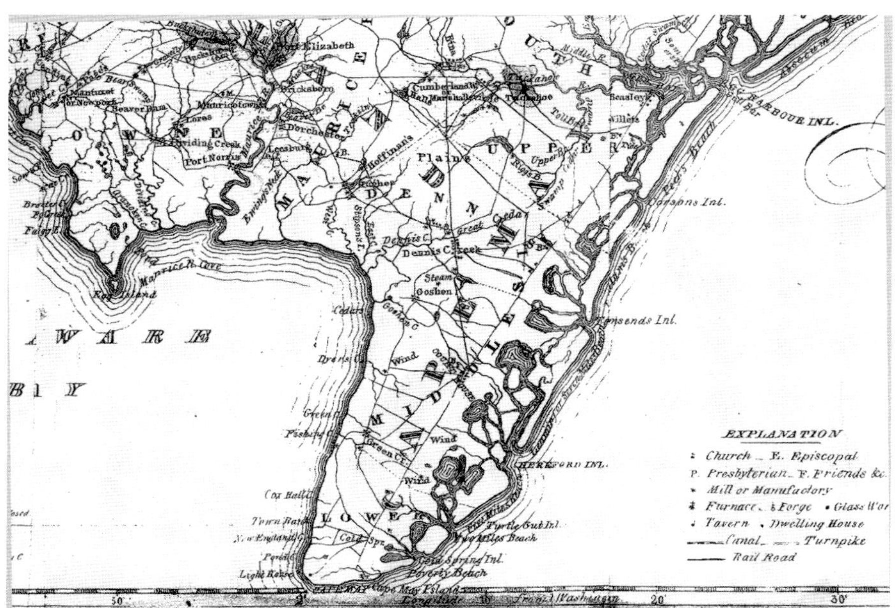

Map of Cape May County and portions of neighboring counties from the Rogers map, 1839. *J.P. Hand collection.*

Despite periods of financial instability in the new republic, life went on as it had for generations. The descendants of the county's whaler-yeomen continued to farm and export livestock, shellfish and timber in various forms. The Cape's shipbuilding industry thrived, and a new industry caught on: tourism based on seaside bathing on Cape Island's pristine beaches. A slow but steady stream of newcomers continued to settle in the county, while many of the descendants of the early families began to migrate to the Midwest, where they purchased more fertile and less expensive farmland.

About thirty years after the Revolution ended, it all began again for the coastal community of Cape May County. On June 18, 1812, President James Madison signed a declaration of war against Great Britain, and the Cape May privateers were back in business, albeit with a new generation of mariner-soldiers.

APPENDIX

Item 1

Agreement between Owners of the State Boat Enterprise
and Captain Elijah Hand

State of New Jersey Cape May County

*Agreement between the owners of the Good Barge
Called the Enterprise and Elijah Hand Captn Viz
That he the Sd Elijah Hand will with the Guard that
is to be Raised by a late Law for the Defence of this
County Enter on board Sd barge and during the time
Of their Service Do the utmost in his Power to Protect
The frontiers of this County and Distress the Enemy
And if by the fortune of war any Prizes fall into
His Hands the Profits arising therefrom to be Equally
Divided according to the Custom of Privateering one
Half to the Captain and his Men and the other Half
To the Owners and it is further agreed between the
Captain and owners that the Wages Allowed by the State
Be the Property of the Men and the Provisions or other
Stores be for the Advantage of the Owners And that
All Prizes that May be taken Shall to the Utmost*

Of his Power without Imbesslement be Sent into
Some Convient Safe Harbour: Any Person
Plundering to lose his whole Share in the Prize
And Make Good all Damages And the Said Captain
Hand Appoint one Person as Lieutenant to have
The Command in his Absence who Shall be Intituled [entitled]
To two Shares, and one Person to Act as Cruise Master
Who Shall have two Shares, That there be four Shares
At the Disposal of the Captain to those who May be
Justly Intituled to them for their Extraordinary Activity
And Merit, the Captain himself to have three Shares

Shares and all the Remainder of the Guard to
Have Each one Share

And the Owners doth further agree that they will
Fit the Said barge in Good order Either to Defend hisself
Or Annoy the Enemy and that if at any time the sd Captain
Shall Inform them of any Repairs being wanted they
Shall be Immediately Had
March 23rd 1782

Elijah Hand Capt

Reeves Iszard	*March 24th X*
John Roberson	*28th*
John Teel	*29*
John Dagg	*29*
Richard Teel	*29 X*
Elijah Hughes	*April 12*
Edward Crowell	*16*
Elijah Smith	*16*
Ephraim Bonde	*April 24*
Daniel Stites	
William Crandel	*24*
Hiram Chester	
George Peck	*27*
Joseph Seley	*April 27*
Jedediah Hughes	*27*

Jeremiah Youngs	*27*
John Daniels	*April 27*
Jeremiah Daniels	*28*
John Nichilson	*31*
John X Jackson	*28*
Benj Taylor	*29*
John Gardner	*29*
Reeves X Richardson	*29*
Daniel Holden	*29*
Daniel Hand	*29*
John X Hand	*29*

[Note: Pension records (1832) show that Captain Elijah Hand's son Recompence Hand as well as Jeremiah Hand, Jacob Garrison, Ezekiel Hand Teal and Alexander Ballard also served on board the *Enterprise.*]

ITEM 2

Privateers of Cape May County in the American Revolution

American privateers played an important role in the fight for Independence. Through the harassment and capture of British merchant vessels, troop transports and Tory vessels, our privateers proved to be a constant annoyance to the British war machine. The captured prizes infused the local economies with much needed cash, supplies and military stores. The vessels themselves were often fitted out as privateers and sent off to capture more prizes.

It is a common myth that our privateers were little more than pirates. Quite to the contrary, our new American government set strict guidelines as to the behavior of the privateers. These included which vessels were fair game, the posting of legal notices advertising the auction of prizes, etc. "Letters of Marque" had to be secured for each privateer vessel by the owners or captains.

The maritime county of Cape May provided a disproportionately high number of privateer captains and crew in relation to its small population and land area. Many Cape May patriots served in the local militias as well as on privateer vessels. Cousins Elijah Hand, Nicholas Stillwell, Enoch

Stillwell and James Willets Jr. all served as militia officers and privateer captains. The list below isn't to be considered a complete accounting of all of Cape May's privateers.

PRIVATEER CAPTAINS	COUNTY TOWNSHIPS
Badcock, John	Upper
Badcock, Joseph	Upper
Bennet, Abraham	Lower (Delaware Bay pilot)
Corson, Darius	Upper
Edwards, Joseph	Upper
Foster, Silas	Lower
Goldin, John	Upper
Griffing, Moses	Upper/Middle
Hand, Elijah	Middle/Downe, Cumberland
Hand, Daniel	Lower
Hughes, Humphrey	Lower (lost at sea in *New Comet* with crew of twenty-five)
Leach, James	?
Schellinger, Enos	Lower (Delaware Bay pilot)
Stillwell, Enoch	Upper/Middle
Stillwell, John	Lower
Stillwell, Nicholas	Upper/Middle
Stites, Israel	Upper
Swain, Aaron	Lower
Taylor, Yelverton	? (Delaware Bay pilot)
Treen, William	Upper
Willets, Enoch	Upper
Willets, Hope	Upper
Willets, James Jr.	Upper

PRIVATEER OWNER/INVESTORS	
Hand, Jesse	Middle
Holmes, John Sr.	Middle
Leaming, Thomas Jr.	Middle/Philadelphia
Stillwell, Enoch	Upper/Middle
Stillwell, Nicholas Jr.	Upper/Middle
Stites, Israel	Upper

Builder of Privateer Vessels
Lee, Abel   Upper

Privateer Officers
Crowell, Elisha   Mate
Hand, Matthew   Second Officer (Delaware Bay pilot)
Holmes, Nathaniel Sr.   Lieutenant
Stites, Israel   Lieutenant
Stites, John   Lieutenant
Taylor, Elias   Mate
Teal, John   Lieutenant

Privateer Crewmen
(This is a partial list and may include crewmen from surrounding counties.)
Bates, Rueben
Bowen, David
Champion, Thomas
Clark, Japhet
Cordrey, Clement
Corson, Jacob
Crawford, Eleazer
Isaac, Crawford   Middle
Foster, Rueben   Lower
Killen, John
Hand, George
Hand, Jeremiah
Hand, Recompence   Middle/Downe, Cumberland County
Hand, T.
Holmes, Nathaniel Sr.   Middle
Marshall, Jeremiah   Upper
Matthews, Elijah   (killed in battle on privateer *Mars*)
McCormick, John
Mulford, William   Lower?
Norbury, Joseph   Middle
Orum, Samuel   Upper
Scull, Isaac   Upper
Seely, David (extra share for being wounded)
Smith, Constantine   Upper/Middle

Snider, John, alias John Taylor   Lower
  ("alias" usually denotes out-of-wedlock birth)
Springer, Thomas   MRT, Cumberland Co.
Steelman, David   GEH, Gloucester Co.
Steelman, Jonathan
Stevens, Henry   Lower
Stillwell, David   Upper
Stites, Daniel   Upper/Middle
Taylor, Mathias
Teal, Ezekiel   Lower
Tilton, Daniel
Townsend, Thomas   Upper
VanGilder, Ezekiel   Upper
Wheaton, Joseph   Upper (crewman or investor?)
Wiley, John   Upper
Willets, Amos   Upper (died on board prison ship in
                          New York)

OFFICERS AND CREW OF THE BARGE, *ENTERPRISE* (NEW JERSEY STATE GUNBOAT)

Information taken from the original, "Agreement between the owners of the Good Barge Called the Enterprise and Elijah Hand Capt.":

Elijah Hand Sr. Capt.

Reeves Izard
John Roberson
John Teel (Lieutenant)
John Dagg
Richard Teel
Elisha Hughes
Edward Crowell
Elijah Smith
Ephraim Bonde
Daniel Stites
William Crandel
Hiram Chester
George Peck
Joseph Seley

Jedediah Hughes
Jeremiah Youngs
John Daniels
Jeremiah Daniels
John Nichilson
John X Jackson (his mark)
Benj Taylor
John Gardner
Reeves X Richardson (his mark)
Daniel Holden
John X Hand (his mark)

ITEM 3

Correspondence between Colonel Elijah Hand and Colonel Charles Mawhood

Perhaps the most celebrated figure from Cape May County during the American Revolution was Colonel Elijah Hand of Fishing Creek, Middle Township. His exploits against the British during the skirmish at Quinton's Bridge and as a privateer captain "cruising" the Delaware Bay and Jersey coast appeared in newspapers throughout the colonies. While Colonel Hand's military prowess was widely reported, he was best known due to the publication of a pair of letters, written a day apart, one addressed to him and the other from him. The first was from the British commander, Colonel Charles Mawhood, demanding that Hand and all of the local militia under his command lay down their arms and return home or face harsh treatment by the British. The second was Colonel Hand's eloquent reply.

The letters first appeared in print about two weeks after they were written, in the *Connecticut Journal* (New Haven) on April 6, 1778. They were printed under the heading:

> *From the* New Jersey Gazette, *To the Printer*
> *I enclose you a copy of Colonel Mawhood's letter to Colonel Hand, and of Hand's answer to his insolent demand, both of which have accidently fallen into my possession, and which I shall be obliged to you for inserting in your paper as Soon as possible.*

It seems that the editor of the *New Jersey Gazette* realized the patriotic and morale-boosting power that Elijah Hand's letter could have on the general population of the colonies. He encouraged editors of newspapers up and down the Eastern Seaboard to publish the letters.

Decades after the war had ended, the letters begin to show up in print again, only then for nostalgic and historic interest. On October 10, 1821, the letters and the story behind them appeared in papers in Charleston, South Carolina, and Pittsfield, Massachusetts. The two letters were reprinted in various papers over the years, and as late as January 3, 1932, the story of the two letters and the skirmish at Quinton's Bridge were published in the *Seattle Daily Times* and the *San Francisco Chronicle*.

Early in the year 1778, British troops under the command of Colonel Charles Mawhood invaded Salem County in search of cattle, horses and any other supplies they could pilfer. On March 18, the British met resistance by the Salem militia, which was dug in along Alloway Creek at Quinton's Bridge. After an initial assault, the British feigned a retreat, and the Salem County men fell for the ploy and charged after the redcoats. The Americans found themselves being fired upon by British regulars well hidden along both sides of the road. Many of the Salem militia were killed or wounded, with the survivors retreating back across Alloway Creek and the relative safety of the trenches.

Hearing of the hostilities, Colonel Hand and his Cumberland boys raced to the scene, and according to Barber and Howe's "Historical Collections of the State of New Jersey" (1844), the following events occurred:

> *Col. Hand of the Cumberland militia, being informed by Col. Holmes that the enemy were in Salem, put his regiment in motion, and was hastening to join Holmes at Quinton's bridge, and by an unforeseen providence, as designed, he arrived there at the very moment when the enemy was dealing death and destruction among our people. Immediately on his arrival, he placed his men in the trenches which our soldiers,* [Salem militia] *had but a little while before left, and opened upon the pursuing enemy such a continued and well-directed fire, as soon put a stop to their career, and saved our people from being cut to pieces. Hand had with him two pieces of artillery, which, when they opened, soon obliged the enemy to face about.*

Three days after his men were repulsed at Quinton's Bridge, Colonel Mawhood ignored Colonel Benjamin Holmes of the Salem militia and wrote directly to Colonel Hand demanding that all local militia officers and men lay down their arms and return home or face dire consequences. Elijah Hand penned his eloquent reply the following day, both of which are shown below.

Colonel Charles Mawhood to Colonel Elijah Hand, March 21, 1778

Colonel Mawhood, commanding a detachment of the British army at Salem, induced by motives of humanity, proposes to the militia at Quintin's Bridge and the neighborhood, as well officers as private men, to lay down their arms and depart, each man to his own home. On that condition, he solemnly promises to re-embark his troops without delay, doing no further damage to the country; and he will cause his commissaries to pay for the cattle, hay, and corn that have been taken, in sterling money.

*If, on the contrary, the militia should be so far deluded, and blind to their true interest and happiness, he will put the arms which he has brought with him into the hands of the inhabitants well affected, called Tories; and will attack all such of the militia as remains in arms, burn and destroy their houses and other property, and reduce them, their unfortunate wives and children, to beggary and distress. And, to convince them that these are not vain threats, he has subjoined a list of the names of such as will be the first objects to feed the vengeance of the British nation.**

Given under my hand, at head-quarters, at Salem, the twenty-first day of March, 1778

**The names given are: Edmund Keasby, Thomas Sinnickson, Samuel Dick, Whitten Cripps, Ebenezer Howell, Edward Hall, John Bowen, Thomas Thomson, George Trenchard, Elisha Cattel, Andrew Sinnickson, Nicholas Kean, Jacob Hufty, Benjamin Holmes, William Shute, Anthony Sharp, and Abner Penton.*

Colonel Elijah Hand to Colonel Charles Mawhood, March 22, 1778

Sir

I have been favored with what you say humanity has induced you to propose. It would have given me much pleasure to have found that humanity had been the line of conduct to your troops, since you came to Salem. Not denying quarters, but butchering our men who surrendered themselves prisoners, in the skirmish at Quinton's Bridge, last Thursday, and bayoneting, yesterday morning, at Hancock's Bridge, in the most cruel manner, in cold blood, men who were taken by surprise, in a situation in which they neither could nor did attempt to make any resistance, and some of whom were not fighting men, are instances too shocking for me to relate, and I hope for you to hear. The brave are ever generous and humane. After expressing your sentiments of humanity, you proceed to make a request, which I think you would despise us if complied with. Your proposal that we should lay down our arms, we absolutely reject. We have taken them up to maintain rights which are dearer to us than our lives; and will not lay them down till either success has crowned our arms with victory, or, like many ancient worthies contending for liberty, we meet with an honorable death. You mention that, if we reject your proposal, you will put arms in the hands of the tories against us. We have no objection to the measure, for it would be a very good one to fill our arsenals with arms. Your threats to wantonly burn and destroy our houses and other property, and reduce our wives and children to beggary and distress, is a sentiment which my humanity almost forbids me only to recite; and induces me to imagine that I am reading the cruel order of a barbarous Attila, and not of a gentlemen, brave, generous, and polished, with a genteel European education. To wantonly destroy will injure your cause more than ours; it will increase your enemies and our army. To destine to destruction the property of our most distinguished men, as you have done in your proposals, is, in my opinion, unworthy a generous foe; and more like a rancorous feud, between two contending barons, than a war carried on, by one of the greatest powers on earth, against a people nobly struggling for Liberty. A line of honour would mark out that these men should share the fate of their country. If your arms should be crowned with victory, (which God forbid!) they and their property will be entirely at the disposal of your Sovereign. The loss of their property, while their persons are out of your power, will only render them desperate; and, as I said before, increase your foes and our army. And retaliation upon tories, and their property, is not entirely out of our power. Be assured that these are the sentiments, and determined resolution, not only of myself only, but of all the officers and privates under me.

My prayer is, sir, that this answer may reach you in health and great happiness.
Given at Head-Quarters, at Quinton's Bridge, the twenty-second day of March 1778.

Elijah Hand, Colonel

Elijah Hand was the son of Recompence Hand and the grandson of Thomas Hand, the whaler. He was born and raised on the bayside at Fishing Creek, Middle Township, and inherited part of his father's plantation there, as well as large tracts of land in Dividing Creek, Cumberland County. His brother Jonathan Hand served as Cape May's representative in the colonial legislature from 1771 to 1776 and in the first state legislature from 1776 to 1778.

Dividing his time between his Cape May and Cumberland plantations, Elijah was elected captain of the Cumberland County militia at Dividing Creek. Later he was promoted to lieutenant colonel and colonel of Cumberland Militia and State Troops. As Captain Hand, he served as master of various privateer vessels and commander of the New Jersey state gunboat. He often cruised and took prizes in tandem with his first cousin Captain Enoch Willets of Upper Township. Elijah's son Recompence served with him on land and at sea.

Like many of Cape May's civilian and military leaders, Elijah Hand didn't long live to see the fruits of his labors. After the war, he returned to his plantation in Cape May County and died before August 31, 1790. He was survived by his wife, Rachel, two sons and a daughter.

ITEM 4

Thomas Leaming Jr. Esq. to William Paterson Esq. 1789

Dear Sir, The Acquaintance I have with you induces me to solicit your Vote and interest to appoint me Prothonotary of the Federal Court in

Pennsylvania, whenever that Court shall be instituted, hoping that I may be deemed capable of serving the office with Propriety, having studied law regularly with the late President Mr Dickinson, was admitted to practice in Pennsylvania, and licensed in New Jersey in 1772—did practice till the courts were stopped by the Revolution, and about 18 months ago resumed it in this City. With respect to Merit shall readily admit that many in the Union have had much more than I, but apprehend many have less in supporting the Measures in favour of the late Revolution, who have been or will be honour'd with Publick employments, which incourages me to make this Application. As you may not have been fully acquainted with my situation or much of my Conduct previous to and during the Revolution, beg leave to give you some account therof a Part of which you will doubtless recollect. After having finished my Studies in Philad I returned to Cape May in order to give some attention to the Affairs of my Father and the Affairs of an Uncle from whom I had some Expectations which both duty and Interest induced me to, as they were both so infirm as not to be able to attend to much Business and living there I practiced the Law 'till the Courts were shut early in the War. I happened to be in Philad when the first Information came of the Battle of Lexington I immediately joined a Company as soon as formed under the then Capt Mifflin & now President of Pennsylvania, in order to have Military Exercise to enable me to instruct the Inhabitants of Cape May: being then fully convinced that the Contest must be determined by the Sword, (and apprehending that the utmost unanimity was especially necssary amongst all the People of America, and that I could be most useful in the County where I resided). As soon as I considered myself capable of giving instruction, I returned to Cape May to endeavor to instruct and unite the People and devoted a very large Share of my Time to Military Duty, serving on Committees & etc : I handed an Association Paper to most of the Inhabitants of Cape May, and had the Pleasure to say, that only one Man in that County refused signing it, and do conclude that much of their Unanimity for which they were so remarkable during the whole War, for altho' a Frontier County, no one of them having joined the Enemy, or were known to be concerned in the New York Trade, was owing to my Exertions. In 1776, you doubtless recollect that I had the Hounour of meeting you in the convention as a deputy from that County, at a Time when the Deputies in a particular Manner risqued every thing that was dear and valuable to Mankind on Earth, for had the British conquered, Halters most likely would have been our Portion. This was a Scene too trying to many good men, as the Enemy had just landed 33,000 Men on Staten Island, as it was said, and the Americans had very few, if any regular Troops in the Field. In this Situation, I most heartily joined you and others in determining to stand or fall with the Liberty of our Country and instructed Congress to declare it Independant. The language being that we had better risqué the Halter, or seek Refuge in the Wilderness among the Savages than submit to Great Brittain. In the Fall of 1776, finding the Enemy were likely to over-run New Jersey, I did not stay there to take the chance of a Protection as many others did, I came to Philad and joined the City Troop of Light Horse, at a time too, when they were much broken up, occasioned by different causes, for when we Marched to Camp only about 12 or 15 Men (besides officers) out of between 40 and 50 went. With this small number I went, and we joined General Washington in the rear of his broken flying Army, in his Retreat near Princetown, Cornwallis then at Kingstown, said to have 10.000 Men & next morning drove us over the Delaware. Our little Troop remained with the General nearly all that Winter, until after the Continental Troops of Regular Horse were formed, when he permitted us to return to Philad. first having offered Commissions in the New Corps to any of us who should chuse to accept them. From that time to this, I have continued in the Philad Troop and never missed a single Tour of Duty, during the War, when called on, in which no Allowance was ever asked by me, or made either for Pay or Horses, and Generally paid our own Expenses. As the War shut up the Courts, I entered into the Mercantile Business in Philada where I settled and have remained ever since (except when the Enemy had it) and did a large share of Business during the Whole Time Continental Money was in Circulation, which I ever gave the fullest Credit to as long as Congress did, being of Opinion that the Fate of the War depended on it; by which I suffered greatly indeed for altho' I had a large sum in Trade, and was very lucky in Arrivals, and also in Privateering (which I considered the most beneficial Way, in which I could serve Myself and the Publick). The Depreciation was so rappid that My Losses were great, and the Publick the only Gainers by my Risque and Exertions, as I was concerned in the Importation of Considerable Quantities of Amunition, Salt, and other Necessaries, and also in the Capture of near 50 Prizes large and small; in which more than 1000 Prisoners were taken, which served to exchange for American

Prisoners in the Hands of the Enemy. By one of the Privateers, which I built and held a Principle share in, about 500 Hessian-English Soldiers were taken in there Vessels within a few Days. This would have been deemed an Acquisition by the Army even if they had lost half the number in affecting it and yet it did not cost the Life of a Man or the Publick, One Shilling. Exclusive of this I was concerned in lending large Sums to the Publick, at different Periods on Loan Office Certificates which by Depreciation was compelled to part with the principal Parts of, at a Loss, and the small sum remaining can now only receive the Interest or in Depreciated Paper, and that only in partial Payments, as is the Case with a considerable Quantity of Provisions which the House I was concerned in, lent out of their own private store for the use of the Army, about the Time of the Revolt, when it was near starving, and the Publick had neither Money or Credit to purchase with, this Provision was designed for the use of our own Vessels, and which we were obliged to replace by paying the cash for—even a higher Price than we were allowed afterwards in certificates, which even now are not worth more than 5 in the Pound. Should you be of Opinion that I am Capable of filling the office and deserve it, as well as any other aplicant, I have to ask you the Favour of your Vote and Interest, promising that if I should be honoured with appointment, that I shall endeavor to do Justice to it. Have to beg you will please acknowledge Receipt of this when at leisure and if you should think Favourable of my Application beg you would inform me (previous to my Appointment to that office being made), of the Time when it is likely to take Place. I'll endeavor to attend the Senate at such a Time concerning that in the Arrangement of the Judicial Department under the new Constitution, suit Court will be instituted and of course suit and Officers must be appointed. Your Complyance will confer the Highest obligations on Sir, your Most Obedient & very Hble Serv. [Humble Servant]
Thomas Leaming Junr
Hon. William Paterson Esq.
Brunswick.

While it is safe to say that Thomas Leaming Jr. had more of an impact on the war effort than any other native of Cape May County, that effect was the result of his efforts in the privateer trade and as an importer of military stores. Leaming was obviously a great self-promoter, as his lengthy letter attests, and some of his claims in the quest for high office can be considered exaggerations. In the beginning of his letter, Leaming gives the impression that he returned to Cape May like a "benevolent father" instructing the simple country folk in the ways of war.

Without questioning his service with Philadelphia's First City Troop and General Washington's army, Leaming's claims concerning his impact on the local militia in his home county are a stretch. Almost since its creation in 1692, Cape May, like the other original counties of New Jersey, fielded a militia made up of local inhabitants who, in turn, elected officers for that militia.

On his return to Cape May from Philadelphia at the beginning of the rebellion, Thomas Leaming Jr. was commissioned adjutant (administrative assistant to the commanding officer) of the Cape May Militia. He ranked just above Quartermaster Nathan Hand and below Major John Hand. The county's highest-ranking field officers during the Revolution, Colonels John Mackey and Nicholas Stillwell, and Lieutenant Colonels Henry Hand and Enoch Stillwell, may have had a different opinion regarding Leaming's influence on their military unit.

It is uncertain as to whether Thomas Leaming received the appointment he sought back in 1789. What is certain is that he died in the yellow fever epidemic of Philadelphia on October 29, 1797.

J.P. Hand

ITEM 5

Instructions to Privateers from Congress 1780–81

In Congress
May 2, 1780
Instructions
To the Captains and Commanders of Private Armed Vessels which shall have Commissions or Letters of Marque and Reprisal

I. You may by force attack, subdue and take all ships and other vessels belonging to the crown of Great Britain, or any of the subjects thereof, on the high seas, or between high and low water marks: (except the ships of vessels, together with their cargoes, belonging to any inhabitant or in habitants of Bermuda, and other such ships and vessels belonging to persons with intent to settle and reside within the United States; which you shall suffer to pass unmolested, the commanders thereof permitting a peaceable search, and giving satisfactory information of the contents of the ladings and destination of the voyages.) And you also may annoy the enemy by all means in your power, by land as well as by water; taking care not to infringe or violate the laws of nations or the laws of neutrality. *This exception is taken away by an ordinance of Congress of March 27th, 1781.*

II. You are to pay a sacred regard to the rights of neutral posers and the usage and custom of civilized nations; and on no pretense whatever, presume to take or seize vessels belong to the subjects of princes or powers in alliance with these United States; except they are employed in carrying contraband goods or soldiers to our enemies; and in such case you are to conform to the stipulations contained in the treaties, subsisting between such princes or powers and these States. And you are not to capture, seize or plunder ships or vessels of our enemies being under the protection of neutral coasts, nations or princes, under the pains and penalties issued by Congress, the ninth day of May, Anno Domini, 1778.

III. You shall bring such ships and vessels as you shall take, with their guns, rigging, tackle, apparel, furniture and ladings to some convenient port or ports; that proceedings may thereupon be had, in due form of law, concerning such captures.

IV. You shall send the master or pilot, and one or more person or persons of the company of every ship or vessel taken by you, in such ship of vessel, as soon after the capture, to be the judge or judges of such court as aforesaid, examined under oath, and make answer to such interrogatories as may be propounded, touching the interest or property of the ship or vessel and her lading. And at the same time you shall deliver or cause to be delivered to the judge or judges all passes, sea-briefs, charter-parties, bills of lading, cockets, letters, and other document or writings found on board; proving the said papers by the affidavit of yourself, or some other person present at the capture; to be produced as they were received, without fraud, addition, subtraction or embezzlement.

V. You shall keep and preserve every ship or vessel and cargo by you taken, until the shall, by sentence of a court, properly authorized, be adjudged lawful prize, or acquitted; not selling, spoiling, wasting or diminishing the same, or breaking the bulk thereof in the ship of vessel you take,—the offender shall be severely punished.

VI. If you, or any of your officers or crew, shall in cold blood kill or maim—or by torture or otherwise cruelly, inhumanely, and contrary to common usage, the practice of civilized nations in war, treat a person or persons surprised in the ship of vessel you shall take---the offender shall be severely punished.

VII. You shall, by all convenient opportunities, send to the Board of Admiralty, written ccounts of the captures you shall make, with the number and names of the captives, and intelligence of what may occur, or be discovered concerning the designs of the enemy, and the destinations, motions, and operations of their fleets and armies.

VIII. One third, at least, of your whole company, shall be land-men.

IX. You shall not ransom or discharge any prisoners or captives; but you are to take the utmost care to bring them into port; and if, from any necessity, you shall be obliged to dismiss any prisoners at sea, you shall, on your return from your cruise, make report thereof, on oath, to the judge of the admiralty, of the state to which you belong, or in deliver, at your expense, or at the expense of your owners, the prisoner you shall bring into port, to a commissary of prisoners, nearest the place of their landing, or into the nearest county-jail.

X. You shall deliver all such further instructions as Congress shall hereafter give in the premises, when you shall have notice thereof.

XI. If you shall do anything contrary to these instruction, or to others to be given, or willingly suffer such thing to be done, you shall not forfeit your commission, and be liable to an action, for breach of the condition of your bond, but be responsible to the party aggrieved for damages sustained by such malversation.

Resolved. *That the Board of Admiralty be empowered and directed to cause to be printed, so many copies of said forms, as they shall judge necessary.*

Resolved. *That the president transmit to the governors of presidents of the respective states, so many copies of said forms, as the Board of Admiralty shall advise; and at the same time inform them, that it is the intention of Congress, that all commissions and instructions now in force, be cancelled as soon as possible, and commissions, bonds and instructions, of the new form be submitted in the pace thereof.*

Extract from the Minutes

Charles Thomson, Secretary

ITEM 6

Report to Congress in 1781 of Conditions of Prison Ships by Messrs. Boudinot, Clymer and Sharpe

General Washington instructed Elias Boudinot, who was at one time president of the Continental Congress and also an attorney who also served as present of the Board of New Jersey Admiralty, to investigate the conditions on British prison ships in New York Harbor. The report was highly critical and highlighted the atrocities committed by the British jailers. Below is an excerpt of Boudinot's report to Congress.

Resolved, That it appears to Congress that a very large number of marine prisoners and citizens of the United States, taken by the enemy, are now close confined on board prison-ships in the harbor of New York.

That the said prison-ships are so unequal in size to the number of prisoners as not to admit of a possibility of preserving life in this warm season of the year, they being crowded together in such a manner as to be in danger of suffocation, as well as exposed to every kid of putrid and pestilent disorder.

That no circumstances of the enemy's particular situation can justify this outrage on humanity, it being contrary to the usage and custom of civilized nations thus deliberately to murder their captives in cold blood, as the enemy will not assert that prison-ships equal to the number of prisoners cannot be obtained so as to afford room sufficient for the necessary purposes of life.

That the enemy do daily improve the distresses to enlist and compel many of our citizens to eurer [?] on board there ships of war, and thus to fight against their fellow citizens and dearest connections.

That the said marine prisoners, until they can be exchanged, should be supplied with such necessities of clothing and provisions as can be obtained to mitigate their present sufferings.

That therefore the Commander-in-Chief be, and is hereby, instructed to the proper officer within the enemy's lines on the said unjustifiable treatment of our marine prisoners, and demand in the most express terms to know the reasons of this unnecessary severity towards them; and that the Commander-in-Chief transmit such answer as may be received theron to Congress, that decided measures for due retaliation may be adopted, if a redress of these evils is not immediately given.

That the Commander-in-Chief be, and is hereby, instructed to direct the supplying of the said prisoners with such provisions and light clothing for their present more comfortable substance as may be in his power to obtain, and in such manner as he may deem most advantageous for these United States.

BIBLIOGRAPHY

Privateers and Maritime History

Burgoyne, B.E. (Translator) *Defeat Disaster and Dedication, The Diaries of the Hessian Officers Jakob Piel and Andreas Wiederhold.* Westminster, MD: Heritage Books, 2008.

Chidsey, Donald Barr. *The American Privateers, A History.* New York: Dodd, Mead & Co. 1962.

Coggeshall, George. *Coggeshall's Voyages Vol. 2.* Leonaur, 2009.

———. *A History of American Privateers and Letters of Marque Interspersed with Several Naval Battles Between American and British Ships of War.* Kessinger Publishing (Reprint), 1856.

Coggins, J. *Ships and Seamen of the American Revolution.* Harrisburg, PA: Promontory Press, 1969.

Dandridge, Danske. *American Prisoners of the Revolution:* Charlottesville VA: The Mitchie Co., 1911.

Donnelly, M.P. and Diehl, D. *Pirates of New Jersey.* Mechanicsburg, PA: Stackpole Books, 2010.

Engle, E. and Lott, A.S. *America's Maritime Heritage.* Annapolis, MD: Naval Institute Press, 1975.

Footner, Hulber. *Soldier of Fortune—The Life and Adventures of Commodore Barney, USN.* Annapolis, MD: Naval Institute Press, 1940.

Garitee, Jerome, R. *The Republic's Private Navy.* Middletown, CT: Wesleyan University Press, 1977.

Jameson, J.F. *St. Eustatius in the American Revolution.* American Historical Review. 8:683–708, 1903.

Knopp, Andre. *One Hundred Year History of the Pilots' Association Bay and River Delaware.* Delaware Heritage Commission, 1996.

Konstam, A., and A. McBride. *Privateers and Pirates—1730–1830.* Botley, UK: Osprey Publishing, Ltd., 2001.

Kurinsky, A. "The Jews of St. Eustatius, Rescuers of the American Revolution," in *Hebrew History Foundation Fact Paper 37.*

Larabee, B.W., W.M. Fowler Jr., E.W. Sloan, J.B. Hattendorf, JJ Safford and A.W. German. *America and the Sea: A Maritime History.* Mystic, CT: Mystic Seaport Museum, 1998.

Lincoln, Charles, H. *Naval Records of the American Revolution 1775–1788 (1906).* Washington, DC: Government Printing Service, 1906.

Lydon, James, G. *Pirates, Privateers and Profits.* Upper Saddle River, NJ: The Gregg Press, 1970.

Maclay, Edgar, S. *A History of American Privateers.* Forgotton Books, 1898.

Mahan, A.T. *The Influence of Sea Power Upon History 1660–1783.* New York: Dover Publications, 1987.

Mitnick, B.J., ed. *New Jersey in the American Revolution.* New Brunswick, NJ: Rivergate Books, 2005.

Patton, Robert H. *Patriot Pirates.* New York: Vintage Books, 2008.

Peterson, Robert A. *Patriots Pirates and Pineys.* Medford, NJ: Plexus Publishing, 1998.

Pierce, Arthur, D. *Smugglers' Woods.* New Brunswick, NJ: Rutgers University Press, 1960.

Scheina, Robert L. "A Matter of Definition: A New Jersey Navy." *American Neptune* (July 1979).

Stark, Francis, R. *The Abolition of Privateering and the Declaration of Paris.* New York: AMS Press, 1967.

Tuchman, Barbara. *The First Salute.* New York: Ballantine Books, 1988.

Wiederholdt, Andreas. *Tagebuch des Capt. Wiederholdt (1776–1780).* Reprinted: Ann Arbor: University of Michigan Library.

Wilbur, C. Keith, MD. *Pirates and Patriots of the Revolution.* Old Saybrook, CT: Globe Pequot Press, 1973.

Cape May History and Genealogy

Dorwart, J.M. *Cape May County, New Jersey.* New Brunswick, NJ: Rutgers University Press, 1992.

Howe, Paul, S. *Mayflower Pilgrim Descendants in Cape May County New Jersey.* Cape May, NJ: A. Hand, 1921.

Stevens, L.T. *The History of Cape May County, New Jersey.* Cape May, NJ: L.T. Stevens, 1897.

Wheeler, E.S. and D.S. Gulick. *Scheyichbi and the Strand of Early Days Along the Delaware.* Reprinted, Philadelphia: Lippincott, 1876.

Wright, F.E. *Colonial Families of Cape May County, New Jersey.* Westminster, MD: Family Line Publications, 1998.

INDEX

ABOUT THE AUTHORS

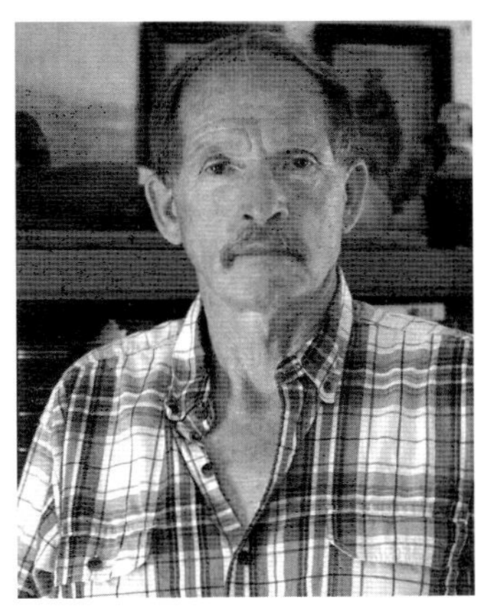

J.P. HAND is a native and lifelong resident of Cape May County, New Jersey. A decoy maker by trade, he has been crafting traditional South Jersey waterfowl carvings for over 47 years. While still in his teens, Jamie was introduced to his family's longtime connection (325 years) to Cape May by an aunt, Ethel Mae Hand Hocker, the family historian of her generation. His passion for the history and culture of Cape May and South Jersey is expressed in the many articles he has written on those subjects.

J.P. Hand is a past president and trustee emeritus of the Cape May County Historical and Genealogical Society and has edited the society's annual journal of history, commonly known as the Blue Book, since 2008. Through that endeavor, he met his coauthor and distant cousin Dr. Daniel Page Stites, with whom he has collaborated on many projects.

He resides with his wife and best friend, Gwen Raring, and their son, Fritz, at Goshen Farm. The farm is located in the heart of Cape May County, a short distance from where many of the events recounted in this work took place.

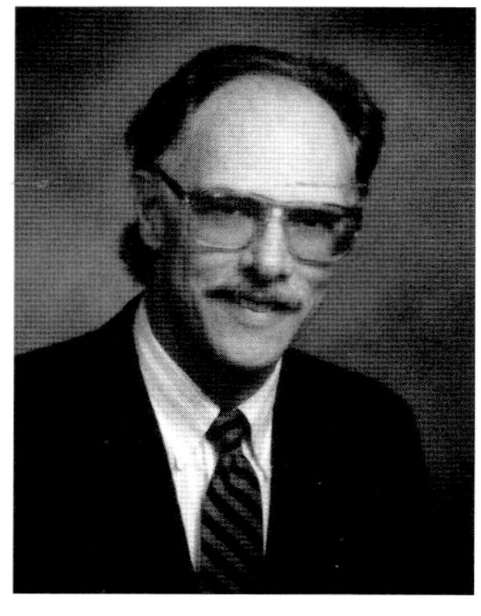

DANIEL P. STITES, MD, grew up in Margate, New Jersey. His father's family immigrated to Cape May County in the seventeenth century. Dan attended Haverford College in Pennsylvania and earned a BA in German. He then went to Stanford Medical School, graduated in 1965 and trained in internal medicine at the University of North Carolina and the National Institutes of Health in Bethesda, Maryland. His career was spent as a medical school professor, researcher, clinician and teacher in the field of clinical immunology at the University of California in San Francisco. His medical career includes the publication of over one hundred journal articles and a number of books on the subject of immunology. He is the fourth great-grandson of Matthew Hand and the third great-grandson of Nathaniel Holmes, both of whom are mentioned in this book. He has written several articles about Cape May history for the *Cape May County Magazine of History and Genealogy*. He lives with his wife, Janice, in Sonoma, California.